Mitri Raheb
Fred Strickert

BETHLEHEM
2000

MITRI RAHEB
FRED STRICKERT

BETHLEHEM 2000

PAST AND PRESENT

PHOTOGRAPHS BY
GARO NALBANDIAN

FOREWORD BY
YASSER ARAFAT

PALMYRA

The Palmyra Publishing House and the authors would like to thank the following people for their assistance and support: Yasser Arafat, Hans-Jürgen Wischnewski, Abdallah Frangi, Axel Burmeister (German Agency for Technical Cooperation), Alice and Norm Rubash (First Presbyterian Church of Evanston), Rainer Zimmer-Winkel, Ismat Amiralai, Barbara Twardon and Klaus Pföhler.

Photo Credits

All photographs by Garo Nalbandian except:
Georg Stein: 60, 63, 74, 89, 92, 93 above,
112 above, 115, 118 below, 121 below right,
124 above, 126, 131, 134, 136, 138, 139, 141
Berliner Missionswerk: 121 below left
Middle East Archive Heidelberg: 105
Matthias Ries: 51 below, 109
Lina Biancorosso: 50 above

German Library
Cataloging in Publication Data

Bethlehem 2000 : past and present / Mitri Raheb
Fred Strickert. Photogr. by Garo Nalbandian
Foreword by Yasser Arafat. - Heidelberg : Palmyra, 1998
Parallelt. in arab. Schr.
Dt. Ausg. u.d.T.: Bethlehem 2000
ISBN 3-930378-21-3

First published 1998
© Copyright of the English edition 1998 by
PALMYRA PUBLISHING HOUSE,
Hauptstraße 64, 69117 Heidelberg, Germany
Telephone 06221/165409, Telefax 06221/167310
e-mail: palmyra-verlag@t-online.de
All rights reserved
Editors: Georg Stein, Christa
Schönrich and Elaine Griffiths
Cover design: Georg Stein
and Annette Künzel
Cover photos: Garo Nalbandian
Typographical design: Christoph Schall
Typesetting and layout: Matthias Ries
Printing and binding:
Freiburger Graphische Betriebe
Printed in Germany
ISBN 3-930378-21-3
A German edition of the
book is also available.

Table of Contents

For a Dialog between Cultures and Religions

Foreword by Yasser Arafat

Palestine is the cradle of the three monotheistic religions, the homeland of the prophets, and the land of peace.

Being the place of birth of Jesus Christ, Bethlehem is one of the most meaningful sites for pilgrimage and tourism in the world. The town is held sacred by all Christians, and also by Jews and Muslims. Religion and history have shaped the contours of Bethlehem to this day.

Yet Bethlehem is also part of a region that has been profoundly marked in the twentieth century by the Israeli-Palestinian conflict. For almost 30 years it suffered Israeli occupation until being placed under the Palestinian Authority in December 1995. Everyday life, however, is still defined by the presence of the occupying forces in the West Bank.

Bethlehem expects four million visitors around the turn of the millennium. The year 2000 will again direct the attention of the world to the place commemorated by the Christian calendar.

Yet the second millennium of the birth of the messenger of peace and love, Jesus Christ, is not only a significant religious occasion. It is also a historical occasion of special significance in religious, historical and cultural terms for the peoples of the Middle East and for the rest of the world. We have dedicated our whole-hearted efforts to achieving the peace we so ardently desire in our country and in the region as a whole. May the celebrations on this important religious and historical occasion provide a unique opportunity to make progress on the road towards reconciliation, coexistence and tolerance between the peoples of the region on the basis of equality and the mutual respect of rights.

These celebrations are, in fact, a chance to renew the spiritual und moral values of all nations in the Middle East and worldwide.

Many other cities in the world are preparing to celebrate the third millennium. Yet no place on earth is as special as Bethlehem, the Palestinian city that was blessed and chosen by God to be the birthplace of the messenger of peace and love, that great event that marked the beginning of the Christian era.

This volume of photos is the first book of its kind about Bethlehem. It gives an impressive picture of the diversity and charm of the town and its environs. History and culture, religion and tourist attractions are given detailed coverage. A lot of space is devoted to the lives of the inhabitants of Bethlehem – their daily life under Israeli occupation and the changes since the beginning of Palestinian self-government in 1995.

The text and photos give a uniquely full view of the town and its people; the reader is taken on a trip to one of the most sacred cities of human history.

I am certain that this book will contribute to promoting a dialog between cultures and religions, a dialog that is the precondition for peace between the peoples of Israel and Palestine.

y. Arafat

Gaza, August 1998

بيت لحم ٢۰۰۰

Captions to the following seven pages.

Page 11: Calligraphy by the Palestinian artist Adel Nasser. The calligraphic text reads: "So the word was made flesh, and dwelt among us, and we beheld his glory, the glory as of the only begotten of the father, full of grace and truth" (John 1:14).

Page 12: Aerial view of Bethlehem. The city is situated 12 kilometers south of Jerusalem at an altitude of 750 m. The road from Jerusalem to Hebron is in the foreground and Beit Sahour, the Judean desert and the Dead Sea are visible in the background.

Page 13: View of Bethlehem from Beit Sahour.

Page 14: Market square in Bethlehem with the bell-tower of the Syrian Orthodox church. Farmers and merchants from all over the region sell their products here.

Page 15: Coffee seller. Drinking coffee plays an important role in Palestinian society. It is a means of communication and a common way of sealing an agreement and marking reconciliation. Preparing and serving coffee is traditionally a male task. One of the older men pours the coffee and the youngest serves it to the guests in the order of their age and status. A common pastime afterwards is telling fortunes from the dregs.

Page 16: Aerial view of Bethlehem. Below, the fortress-like structure around the Church of the Nativity and Manger Square. Beit Sahour (including the Shepherds' Fields) and the Judean desert are situated east of Bethlehem.

Page 17: Churches and mosques in the light of the setting sun. Left to right: the Syrian Orthodox church, the minaret of the Mosque of Omar, the Lutheran Christmas Church and the bell-tower of the Armenian monastery.

CHAPTER I

The Town of Bethlehem: Past and Present

*O little town of Bethlehem,
how still we see thee lie!
Above thy deep and dreamless sleep
The silent stars go by;
Yet in thy darkness shineth
The everlasting light.
The hopes and fears of all the years
Are met in thee tonight.*

Bethlehem is no longer the quiet little town of the Christmas carol. Today it is a bustling city of 40,000 inhabitants, merging without boundary into the neighboring towns of Beit Sahour and Beit Jala. When Joseph and Mary made their nocturnal visit Bethlehem was only a village, with a population that has been estimated at between 300 and 1,000 inhabitants.

Bethlehem lithography by David Roberts (1839).

Left: Christmas celebration in Bethlehem. Photograph from the early twentieth century.

The Name Bethlehem

The name of this place may originally have derived from *Lachma,* the Mesopotamian god of vegetation and fertility known from the creation story *Enuma Elish.* Bethlehem was known to all cultures as a place of fertility and growth. Even the Romans established a cult of Adonis in a grove near the Grotto of the Nativity . In the Old Testament, this was reflected in the name of the region *Ephrata,* which also means *fertile.*

Bethlehem is a Hebrew word and is the name used in the Bible. Today's residents use the Arabic name *Beit Lachem. Beth* and *Beit* mean *house. Lachem* refers to *meat. Lehem* refers to *bread.* Hence the meaning *House of Bread* or *House of Meat.*

The name of this city suggests a place where the stranger is welcomed and where there is food in abundance, even amidst the rugged desert landscape.

In the last two millennia people have come to Bethlehem for a different kind of food, nourishment for the soul. Jerome recorded the words of the Roman noblewoman Paula who came to Bethlehem in the late fourth century:

> *Hail Bethlehem, House of Bread,*
> *wherein was born that bread*
> *that came down from heaven.*
> *Hail Ephrata, land of fruitfulness and of fertility,*
> *whose fruit is the Lord himself.*

Farmers, merchants and pilgrims in the square in front of the Church of the Nativity. Photograph from the second half of the nineteenth century.

بيت لحـم ٢٠٠٠

View of the Church of the Nativity from the north. The oldest city gate of Bethlehem is situated to the far right. Photograph from the second half of the nineteenth century.

Bethlehem today is famous for its Arab hospitality, for its warm, friendly welcomes, and for its variety of delicious food.

Bethlehem: Historical Survey

Bethlehem's story begins some 50,000 years ago when this area served as a land bridge between Africa, Asia, and Europe. At that time various species of animals wandered back and forth between the continents. In the twentieth century farmers digging a cistern some 15 meters below the surface found the bones of some of them, including remnants of panthers, elephants, hippopotami, rhinos, giraffes, and antelopes. The markings on bones from flint tools indicate an early human occupation of the area, which is corroborated by discoveries in the caves that dot the surrounding hillsides.

Bethlehem itself is located at one of the highest points of the area, some 750 meters above sea level on the edge of the watershed. Its early settlement seems to have resulted from its position bordering the fertile areas of Beit Sahour and Beit Jala, and the Judean desert to the south and east.

Archaeological excavations have uncovered Bronze Age finds from 5,000 years ago in nearby Beit Sahour and Iron Age finds from 3,000 years ago elsewhere in the vicinity, including the area just to the east of the Church of the Nativity.

Some scholars believe they have found a reference to Bethlehem among the Amarna letters in Egypt (fourteenth century B.C.).

King Abdi-Hepa of Jerusalem refers to a nearby place called *Bit-Nin-Urta*, possibly another way of speaking about the home of a fertility god like *Lachma*.

According to the Old Testament Book of Ruth, the first known residents were a couple named Elimelech and Naomi. About 3,200 years ago, they lived in a simple farming village struggling to survive in the midst of famine. This house of nourishment had become barren, and so they sojourned for a time in Moab, east of the Dead Sea. Their story is short, but their memory lives on and so does the family name in the story of their Moabite daughter-in-law Ruth and her quest to establish roots by gathering sheaves of barley in the fields of Boaz near Beit Sahour.

This hillside village was also home to shepherds, including Ruth's grandson Jesse and his eight sons from the tribe of Judah. The prophet Samuel graced the town of Bethlehem with his presence in his search for a new king of Israel. The lot fell to the youngest of those sons, David, who chose Jerusalem – only nine kilometers away – as his capital to avoid the impression of favoritism, and there he established a dynasty.

During this early period of history, one of the central characteristics of Bethlehem was its mixed population and mutual tolerance among people of different ethnic, religious, and cultural backgrounds. This is most poignantly expressed in the immortal words of Ruth, the Moabite, who found hospitality among the people of Bethlehem:

> *Where you go, I will go;*
> *Where you lodge, I will lodge;*
> *Your people shall be my people,*
> *And your god shall be my god (1:16).*

Yet the story of Ruth is not an isolated case. One of the famous judges of Israel was a man from Bethlehem named Ibzan, who was known for encouraging his own children to be open to such intermarriage. David's own sister Abigail is said to have married Jether, an Ishmaelite. When things became difficult for David's family, he sent them to Moab, the land of his grandmother Ruth, to seek refuge.

At the end of the tenth century B.C., King Rehoboam fortified Bethlehem and made it a store city for food, oil, and wine. Yet for 1,000 years Bethlehem remained a quiet little town in the shadow of Jerusalem. At the end of the sixth century B.C., only 123 exiles from Babylon returned home to settle in Bethlehem. Yet the prophet Micah saw promise in spite of the small number of returnees:

> *But you, O Bethlehem of Ephrata,*
> *Who are one of the little clans of Judah,*
> *From you shall come forth for me*
> *One who is to rule Israel,*
> *Whose origin is from of old,*
> *From ancient days (5:1).*

So, according to the New Testament, during a census carried out under Roman occupation, Joseph and Mary made their way to this seemingly insignificant village, like many with family roots in Bethlehem. Here the birth of Jesus took place and the shepherds and wise men paid their visits. Shortly after, Bethlehem suffered the tragedy of a paranoid ruler who, on hearing rumors of this birth, had every young boy killed.

The evangelist Matthew was aware of the significance that Jesus' birth would have for this town and therefore quoted the words of Micah – but with one change:

> *And you, Bethlehem in the land of Judah,*
> *Are by no means least among*
> *The rulers of Judah;*
> *For from you shall come a ruler*
> *Who is to shepherd my people Israel (2:6).*

Right: Palestinian family from Bethlehem. Photograph from the second half of the nineteenth century.

بيت لحـــم ٢٠٠٠

Bethlehem: A Chronology

50 000 B.C.	Prehistorical settlement in Bethlehem		313	Emperor Constantine issues Edict of Toleration
2000 B.C.	Canaanite town		326	Helen visits Bethlehem to commission church
1400 B.C.	Possibly mentioned in Amarna letters		386	Jerome arrives in Bethlehem
1200 B.C.	Settlement of Tribe of Judah begins		483	Mar Sabas establishes monastery
1150 B.C.	Story of Ruth		614	Persian invasion
1008 B.C.	Prophet Samuel anoints David		637	Caliph Omar visits Bethlehem
586 B.C.	Babylon destroys Jerusalem		1100	Baldwin I crowned king of Crusader Kingdom
539 B.C.	Cyrus of Persia begins rule		1291	Egyptian Mamelukes begin rule
333 B.C.	Alexander the Great		1516	Ottoman Turks begin rule
303 B.C.	Egyptian Ptolemies begin rule		1920	British Mandate begins
198 B.C.	Seleucids of Antioch begin rule		1948	West Bank becomes part of the Hashemite Kingdom of Jordan
164 B.C.	Judas Maccabeus defeats Seleucids		1967	Israeli army occupies the West Bank and Bethlehem
63 B.C.	Roman Pompey conquers Jerusalem			
4 B.C.	Birth of Jesus		1987	Intifada begins
70	Romans destroy second Jerusalem temple		1995	Palestinian autonomy comes to Bethlehem
135	Hadrian defeats Bar-Cochba and expels Jews			

Surprisingly to the modern reader, the New Testament virtually ignores the history of Bethlehem except for a few chapters relating the birth of Jesus. Yet there must have been some sort of early Christian community residing in this city, since one of the first popes, Evaristus by name (100-109), is said to have had a gentile mother and a Jewish father from Bethlehem. The second-century Christian writer from Nablus, Justin Martyr, was already aware of traditions associating Jesus' birth with a cave near Bethlehem.

Physically, the town remained small and insignificant. During the Bar-Cochba revolt of 132-135 it was devastated by the Roman army under Hadrian, and its Jew-ish residents were expeled from the area. Tertullian tells us that Bethlehem was entirely gentile at the beginning of the third century. At this time Roman soldiers who built the nearby aqueduct made Bethlehem a cult center for the fertility god Adonis. Jerome described the situation with the following words:

From Hadrian's time until the reign of Constantine, for about 180 years, the Gentiles used to worship an image of Jupiter, set up in the place of the resurrection, and on the rock of the cross a marble statue of Venus... Bethlehem, now ours and the earth's most sacred spot... was overshadowed by a grove of Tammuz, which is

*Adonis, and in the cave where the infant Mes-
siah once cried, the paramour of Venus was be-
wailed.*

Not until 326 and the visit of Helen, the mother of the first Christian emperor Constantine, did Bethlehem achieve an important physical presence with the construction of a church on the site of the nativity.

Shortly thereafter, Bethlehem flourished as a center for the growing monastic movement. The first arrival was Jerome, who resided in Bethlehem from 386-420 and founded western biblical study with his translation of the Bible into the Latin *Vulgate*. At the same time, the Roman noblewoman Paula and her daughter Eustochium came to the region and used their fortune to build the first monasteries and a hospice for pilgrims. Then followed the great leaders Chariton, Theodosius, and Sabas so that soon the nearby desert was blooming with over 100 monasteries.

As evidence of Bethlehem's rise in importance, the Roman emperor Justinian in the beginning of the sixth century provided funds for the fortification of walls and the embellishment of the town through the building of churches including the reconstructed basilica. Arculfus, a seventh-century pilgrim from western Europe, left this written description of the town:

> *Bethlehem is situated on a narrow ridge sur-
> rounded on all sides by valleys, which stretches
> from east to west for about a mile.*
> *Round the level plateau on the top of it is a low
> wall without towers, built on the very brow of
> the hill, overlooking the valleys that lie about it
> on either side. In the middle space between the
> walls the citizens straggle along the long axis.*

This was followed by various waves of newcomers to the area: the Persians (614), Muslim Arabs (637), Christian Crusaders (1099), Egyptian Mamelukes (1291), and the Ottoman Turks (1516).

On Christmas Day in 1100, Baldwin I was crowned in Bethlehem as the first king of the Latin Kingdom of Jerusalem. Within several years Bethlehem was raised in status to a bishopric.

A significant stage of the building activities was dominated by the Crusaders. By the end of the fifteenth century, it was a strong fortified city with walls and moats punctuated by two massive towers – one on the western hill and the other near the basilica.

The fortifications were razed by the Ottoman conquerors, so that Bethlehem was once again a tiny, insignificant village for nearly 400 years. Twentieth-century world politics continued to play havoc with the residents of Bethlehem as occupation passed from the hands of the Ottomans to the British Mandate to the West Bank of the Hashemite Kingdom of Jordan to Israeli military administration.

During the most recent period of history under Israeli occupation, the Palestinians went through several phases: from non-cooperation to maintenance of the status quo to isolation and finally to active resistance. The *Intifada*, the uprising, which, corresponding to the literal meaning of the word, has in fact led to *a shaking off* of the Israeli occupation, lasted from 1987 until 1994.

In spite of the struggle which has characterized it, the twentieth century has been for Bethlehem a time of unparalleled growth. The city limits moved outward in all directions, and the number of residents increased to fill this modern city. The population of the Bethlehem district reached 138,918 in 1992. It is estimated to stand at 184,000 by the year 2000.

On December 21, 1995, when the green, red, black, and white Palestinian flag was officially raised in Manger Square, Bethlehem began a new era marked by the sincere longing for a long-lasting and comprehensive peace and for extensive regional coexistence and development. These hopes and dreams are symbolized for all Palestinians by the slogan *Bethlehem 2000.*

CHAPTER II

The Church of the Nativity

The Church of the Nativity is one of the oldest church buildings in the world. Even more significant is the fact that it has been in continuous use since the present structure was built by Emperor Justinian in the early sixth century.

The first permanent structure was one of three churches built by Emperor Constantine in the early fourth century, after Christianity achieved the status of a recognized religion in the Roman Empire. Bishop Macarius of Jerusalem had issued this request when he traveled to Nicea to take part in the first ecumenical council in 325.

In 326 Constantine's mother, Helen, traveled to the Holy Land and investigated the sites most important in the life of Christ.

Helen was shown a cave outside the city of Bethlehem, where early traditions of the Christian community had localized the place of Jesus' birth. The Gospel of Luke reports that Jesus was born in a manger because there was no room in the inn. The Gospel of Matthew mentions a house where Joseph and Mary were staying when the Magi arrived. However, the second-century Palestinian writer Justin Martyr noted that this manger was located in a cave.

Many local shepherds customarily kept their flocks in caves at night. In fact, traditional Palestinian houses were often built over caves. Usually houses consisted of a single room which was used for eating, sleeping, and social gatherings. It was often subdivided into levels with the lower one reserved for animals. So Luke's comment that Joseph and Mary could find "no room in the inn" may refer to the crowded upper level, which means that they may have found a place in the lower level with the animals. The commonly held idea of the manger as a barn is more Western in origin.

Jerome states that the Roman cult of Adonis was later established in a grove near this place and that rites continued to be practiced in the cave throughout the second and third centuries. Yet Origen of Caesarea ac-

Left: Greek Orthodox monks in front of the entrance to the Church of the Nativity. The low door stems from Ottoman times. In the sixteenth century the main entrance was made smaller in order to prevent horse- and camel-riders from entering; the fortress-like building could also be defended more easily.

Chronology of the Church of the Nativity

4 B.C.	*Birth of Jesus*
326	*Visit of Helen to Bethlehem*
334-339	*Building of the Church of the Nativity during the reign of Emperor Constantine*
386	*Jerome arrives in Bethlehem*
529	*Church of the Nativity destroyed in a Samaritan riot*
540	*Justinian rebuilds Church of the Nativity*
1130	*Date on column painting*
1169	*Date on wall mosaics inscription*
1670	*Ceiling repaired and iconostasis built*
1880	*St. Catherine's Church enlarged*
1934	*Modern archaeological survey and repair*
1997	*Proposal for modern renovations*

View of the Church of the Nativity with its five naves from the bell-tower of the Greek Orthodox monastery. Behind it, to the north, lies the Franciscan St. Catherine's Church.

Right: The "Christmas bells" of the Greek Orthodox monastery.

cepted the historical authenticity of this location, which was preserved among the well-known traditions of the people of Bethlehem. Unlike other events in Jesus' life, for which a variety of sites have been given, no alternative location has ever been established for his birth.

The focus of the church of Constantine was an octagonal structure with an opening looking down into the cave. To its west was a large basilica and then an atrium lined with columns which opened in the direction of the town of Bethlehem.

Justinian's sixth-century renovations included an enlarged basilica and the addition of three apses where the octagonal structure once stood. Access to the grotto was made easier by stairways so that worshippers could meditate there on the meaning of the incarnation.

One of the first views of Bethlehem for many visitors is the familiar site of the facade at the entryway to the Church of the Nativity. In some ways it gives a complicated and cluttered impression. In other ways, though, it reveals a historical development which emphasizes the continued occupation of this same ancient edifice through successive stages, each representative of different peoples, different cultural attitudes, and different times.

Three stages of the doorway are evident today. The upper lintel gives a faint reminder of the three-meter-wide Justinian entrance which was flanked by two other doors. Traces of the north door emerge from behind the eighteenth-century buttressing while the south door is lost behind the wall of the Armenian monastery. The lower pointed arch comes from Crusader times when the wall needed strengthening and when architectural styles stretched heavenward. Finally, the present narrow door, erected in the Ottoman period to prevent the entry of the travelers' horses and camels, compels the visitors to stoop in humility when entering this historic holy structure.

Still resting against the wall are pieces of broken columns and bases taken from the atrium of Constantine's time. The grandeur of mosaics, marble, and gilded decoration has long disappeared, and in its place we now find a dark and well-worn memorial for the humblest of births.

Page 30: Greek Orthodox monks during a procession in the Church of the Nativity.

Page 31: The monolithic pillars in both side naves of the Church of the Nativity are of reddish limestone and bear Corinthian capitals. Their bases are hidden by the raised floor.

Page 32 above: The main nave of the Church of the Nativity with the altar. In the center, the mosaic floor from pre-Justinian times.

Page 32 below: Gold-colored wall mosaics in the clerestories of the main nave.

Above: Twelfth-century saint's image on one of the 5.50-meter limestone pillars.

Decorative Art

T oday the wall mosaics are in a ruined and fragmentary state. Visitors are sometimes disappointed by the dark interior of the church, which is not very impressive at first sight. Yet the message of the artists continues to speak across the ages.

On the first Christmas, the heavenly angels proclaimed "good news for all people". As a reminder, angels in mosaic decorated the upper portions of the basilica between the windows. The artist Basil's signature, both in Latin and in Syriac, is a reminder of the building's multinational character.

Most of these nave decorations were completed in the twelfth century in a Latin Crusader church by an Eastern emperor, Manuel Comnenus. His goal was nothing less than the reunification of a church split by earlier schisms. Thus portrayal of seven ecumenical councils and six local councils recalls the depth of theological heritage. The parade of saints preserved on columns reminds visitors of the variety and richness of gifts offered by Christians from Norway to Arabia, providing a balanced picture of the contributions of East and West, North and South.

With all the diversity of images, the focus remains on the Christ-child. His rich heritage of Old Testament ancestry branches out from the tree of Jesse. The whole decorative program moves the visitor forward through the long, narrow nave to the unifying simple grotto.

The only decorations remaining from the pre-Justinian church are the mosaics underneath the present floor. Unlike the pictures on the wall which stem from a later period and display human themes, the geometric figures of the floor mosaics are a reminder of the Judeo-Christian view, which was adopted and further developed in Islamic art. This tradition refrained from using such images and sought to express the boundless eternal ideas in interlocking and endless abstractions.

The silver star in the marble-lined Grotto of the Nativity. It bears the inscription: Hic de Virgine Maria Jesus Christus natus est (Here the Virgin Mary gave birth to Jesus Christ). The 15 lamps above the star represent the different Christian denominations.

Announcement of the Birth of Jesus

Gospel of Luke 1:26-38

In the sixth month the angel Gabriel was sent by God to a town in Galilee called Nazareth, to a virgin engaged to a man whose name was Joseph, of the house of David. The virgin's name was Mary. And he came to her and said, "Greetings, favored one! The Lord is with you."

But she was much perplexed by his words and pondered what sort of greeting this might be. The angel said to her, "Do not be afraid, Mary, for you have found favor with God. And now you will conceive in your womb and bear a son, and you will name him Jesus. He will be great, and will be called the Son of the Most High, and the Lord God will give him the throne of his ancestor David. He will reign over the house of Jacob forever, and of his kingdom there will be no end." Mary said to the angel, "How can this be, since I am a virgin?" The angel said to her, "The Holy Spirit will come upon you, and the power of the Most High will overshadow you; therefore the child to be born will be holy; he will be called Son of God... For nothing will be impossible with God." Then Mary said, "Here am I, the servant of the Lord; let it be with me according to your word."

Luke 2:1-7

In those days a decree went out from Emperor Augustus that all the world should be registered. This was the first registration and was taken while Quirinius was governor of Syria. All went to their own towns to be registered. Joseph also went from the town of Nazareth in Galilee to Judea, to the city of David called Bethlehem, because he was descended from the house and family of David. He went to be registered with Mary, to whom he was engaged and who was expecting a child. While they were there, the time came for her to deliver her child. And she gave birth to her firstborn son and wrapped him in bands of cloth, and laid him in a manger, because there was no place for them in the inn.

Quran, Sura 19: Miriam

Recite the account of Mary according to this Book, when she withdrew from her people to a place towards the east, and screened herself off from them. Then we sent our angel to her and he appeared to her in the form of a well proportioned man. On perceiving him she exclaimed: "I seek refuge with the Gracious One from you if you are at all righteous." The angel reassured her, "I am but a messenger from your Lord, that I may give you tidings of a righteous son who will grow to maturity." She marveled: "How shall it be that I shall have a grown son, seeing that no man has touched me and I have not been unchaste?" The angel said, "So it is, but your Lord says, 'It is easy for me.' It is so ordained that we may make him a sign unto people and a source of our mercy. This has been decreed."

So she conceived him, and withdrew with him to a remote place. When her time came the pains of childbirth drove her to the trunk of a palm tree. Realizing her condition, she cried out, "Would that I had died before this and had been quite forgotten." The voice of the angel reached her from below, "Grieve not, for the Lord has provided a stream below you, wherein you may wash yourself and the child. Then take hold of the branch of the palm tree and shake it. It will shed fresh ripe dates upon you. Thus eat and drink and wash and be at rest."

The Church of the Nativity displays the approach to worship within the Greek Orthodox tradition. Prominent is the iconostasis, or icon screen, which separates the congregation from the Holy of Holies and the mysteries of God, following the Old Testament temple as a prototype. It differs, however, from that tradition in that it opens to the people at the reading of the Gospel. The standard icons, which are seen not merely as simple pictures, but rather as windows to God, are where the worshipper finds communion with the divine. The Eastern aesthetic features adornment through the multiplicity of images and their enhancement by the use of gold and silver. This idea of worship can be summarized in the words of the Russian theologian Nicolas Zernov:

The Oriental liturgy is the foundation of inspiration of the Oriental Christians. The liturgy appeals to all the human senses; the eyes of the faithful admire the beauty of the holy icons. Their ears listen to hymns. The incense surrounds them with aromatic perfume, the body glorifies the Creator with symbolic acts and the spirit is elevated for the adoration of the heavenly Father.

St. Catherine's Catholic Church, built on the foundations of the Monastery of St. Jerome, displays the approach to worship from the Latin Western perspective. The altar, where the Mass takes place, is prominent. The Western aesthetic values simplicity, openness, and light. The worshipper contemplates the wonder of God from a distance, but comes forward to share in the eucharistic communion.

Left and below: Armenian Christians at prayer in front of the Nativity Altar. On the right-hand side both pictures show the Altar of the Magi (the Three Kings).

Page 38: The Greek Orthodox patriarch in the Grotto of the Nativity at Christmas.

Page 39: Greek Orthodox monks at prayer in front of the iconostasis.

Grotto of St. Jerome

*O*ne of the most important theologians in the history of the church lived for 34 years in Bethlehem. This was Jerome, who had left Rome during the invasion of the Visigoths in 384 and came to Bethlehem in 386. He dedicated his life to severe discipline and acts of penance in the monastic life. As a Latin scholar and theologian he did much to bridge the gap between the western and eastern branches of the church.

In the context of Jerome's involvement in theological discussion and writing, his main contribution was the critical study of Latin biblical manuscripts and a comparison with the original Hebrew and Greek texts. As a result, he produced the Latin edition of the Bible, the Vulgate, which remained the authoritative version in the Latin church until the Second Vatican Council in 1962-1965.

Jerome was joined in Bethlehem by a Roman noblewoman named Paula and her daughter Eustochium. As a descendant from the leading Gracchi and Scippio families of Rome, she used her wealth to build a monastery for Jerome and his followers. She built a second convent for many sisters who followed her example by leaving the patrician society of Rome for the spiritual life of Bethlehem. They also established a hospice for pilgrims.

Underneath the north apse of the Church of the Nativity is the Grotto of St. Jerome, where Jerome and Paula were buried. Earlier burials from the first and second centuries attest to an early recognition of the importance of this site.

Pilgrims

*B*ishop Eusebius, who chronicled Constantine's deeds in building the Church of the Nativity, recognized that this edifice would have a profound effect on Palestine "since it was from that source that the river of life flowed forth to mankind". With the building of churches, the age of pilgrimage began. From this point, the land was often considered the fifth gospel and the expression "The Holy Land" became common.

Over the centuries, thousands of Christians have made pilgrimages to Bethlehem, and now, at the end of the second millennium, visitors come from all over the world. Today tourism is one of the largest industries in the Middle East.

Pilgrim's cross on one of the monolithic pillars.

Chronology of Pilgrims

Report by Pilgrim Otto von Neuhaus (1333)

In one day I reached the holy town of Bethlehem, which cannot be considered the least among the first. The way is very pretty in places and partly wooded. At the birthplace of the light of the world a very sacred and lovely church has been built, fairly large; it is covered with lead and adorned with marble work and paintings depicting the ancestry of Christ. I do not think I have ever seen so lovely a church anywhere in the world. It was well protected with walls, towers and outwork. Bethlehem is small in area and confined on both sides, made safe by deep valleys. Its inhabitants are mostly Christians, albeit schismatics, and the area produces a lot of excellent wine.

Altar with iconostasis in the Church of the Nativity. Lithography by David Roberts (1839).

Letter of Jerome to the Roman Noblewoman Marcella (386)

Time forbids me... to recount the bishops, the martyrs, the divines who have come to Jerusalem from a feeling that their devotion and knowledge would be incomplete and their virtue without the finishing touch, unless they adored Christ in the very spot where the Gospel first flashed from the gibbet...

Every man of note... hastens hither... They all assemble here and exhibit in this one city the most varied of virtues. Differing in speech, they are one in religion, and almost every nation has a choir of its own.

As everyone praises most what is within his reach, let us pass now to the cottage-inn which sheltered Christ and Mary. With what words and what expressions can we set before you the cave of the Savior?

Behold in this poor crevice of the earth the Creator of the heavens was born; here He was wrapped in swaddling clothes; here He was seen by the shepherds; here He was pointed out by the star; here He was adored by the wise men. This spot is holier, I think, than that Tarpian rock [upon which the Temple of Jupiter was founded in Rome] which has shown itself displeasing to God by the frequency with which it has been struck by lightning.

Pilgrimage of the Russian Abbot Daniel (1106/1107)

I, Daniel, an unworthy Abbot of Russia, the least among the monks, ill at ease by reason of my many sins and the insufficiency of my good works, was seized first with the idea, and then with an impatient yearning to behold the sacred city of Jerusalem and the Promised Land...

I have written this [journal] for the faithful, so that, in hearing the description of the holy places, they might be mentally transported to them, from the depths of their souls, and thus obtain from God the same reward as those who have visited them.

Many virtuous people, by practicing good works and charity to the poor, reach the holy places, without leaving their homes, and so render themselves worthy of a greater recompense from our God and Savior Jesus Christ. Others, of whom I am the chief, after having visited the holy city of Jerusalem and the holy places, pride themselves as if they had done something meritorious, and thus lose the fruit of their labor. And again, others who have made the pilgrimage, return without having seen many valuable things, so eager were they to return home; for this journey cannot be made quickly, nor can all the holy places in Jerusalem and other localities be hurried through.

Pilgrims in front of the Church of the Nativity. Photograph from the end of the nineteenth century.

A Description by Ida Pfeiffer from Vienna (June 1842)

The church is near the town, built on the very spot where Christ was born. The whole complex is ringed by a fortress wall, through which leads a low, narrow door. In front of the fortress is a fine, well-paved square. On entering through the little doorway you immediately come into the lobby or actually the nave of the church, which is unfortunately half ruined, but which may have been one of the finest and largest ever. You can still see traces of mosaics on the walls. Two rows of beautiful tall pillars, 44

in all, divide the interior, and the rafters, said to be made of cedar of Lebanon, look new. Under the high altar of this great church lies the grotto in which Christ was born. There are two stairways leading to it, one belonging to the Armenians and the other to the Greeks. The Latins lost out. The walls and floor are marble-clad. A marble slab marks the spot from which emanated the true light. A radiant sun behind this slab receives its light from the many ever-burning lamps.

Chapter III

Christianity in Bethlehem

Palestinian Christianity

With the coming of the Holy Spirit at Pentecost, the church was born in Palestine. Since then, there has been a continuing presence of Christianity in Bethlehem. During the first centuries, the local church has kept alive the memory of Jesus' birth in Bethlehem, as Justin Martyr and Origen attest. Later, when Bethlehem fell under the sway of one national power or an-

other, the local church provided continuity for worship, even at times when unfavorable circumstances demanded perseverance. Throughout this 2,000-year-old history, the local Christians continued to acculturate themselves to an ever-changing context: Syrian, Roman, Greek, Arab – to name but a few. Today a strong indigenous church has emerged, with a gifted and dedicated leadership so that pastors, priests, sisters, teachers, and administrators are nearly all Palestinian.

Page 44: View from the Church of the Nativity. The two men belong to the guard of honor of the Greek Orthodox patriarch.

Above: Syrian Orthodox priest with Aramaic bible

Left: Christian girl from Bethlehem.

Armenian Christmas service with the Armenian patriarch and the mayor of Bethlehem, Hanna Nasser.

Christian Communities
in Bethlehem

Christianity in Palestine was characterized from the beginning by its diversity. Since the first century, various Christian communities have co-existed in the Holy Land. Today the challenge is to celebrate unity in diversity.

Pentecost marks the birth of the church and, therefore, the church of Jerusalem is considered to be the mother of all churches. There has been a continuous Christian presence in Palestine ever since.

The Greek Orthodox Patriarchate in Jerusalem is the oldest ecclesiastical institution in the Holy Land, having been instituted at the Council of Chalcedon in 451.

It is also one of the oldest churches in Bethlehem. The Greek Orthodox Church in Bethlehem today has 2,000 members and is the seat of the bishopric.

The establishment of the Greek Catholic Church in the Holy Land goes back to the seventeenth century and was the result of Roman Catholic missionary work among the Greek Orthodox Christians. The name Greek Catholic shows the identity of this church, retaining the Byzantine liturgy of the Greek Orthodox Church while entering into union with Rome. Therefore, it was recognized as an autonomous patriarchate. The Greek Catholic Church in Bethlehem was dedicated in 1964 and has around 500 members.

It was in 301, almost 20 years prior to the Constantine era, that Armenia declared Christianity its state religion. Armenian pilgrims started coming to the Holy Land in the fourth century, and a permanent community struck root in Jerusalem. In 1337 the Armenian Patriarchate was established in Jerusalem, and an Armenian community has existed in Bethlehem since the Middle Ages. Although the Jerusalem Armenian community grew substantially in the twentieth century – partly as a result of migrations away from the massacres of the Ottoman empire – the Bethlehem community is made up of only around 40 families today.

The history of the Evangelical Lutheran Church in the Holy Land started in the year 1841, when an Anglo-Prussian bishopric was founded in Jerusalem. The second bishop Samuel Gobat, with a Swiss Reformed background, was nominated by the King of Prussia, Frederick William IV, and installed by the Archbishop

of Canterbury. While he is mostly remembered for the Bishop Gobat School in Jerusalem, he also founded a Protestant school in Bethlehem in 1854. In 1860 a chapel was built for the growing congregation. The present Evangelical Lutheran Christmas Church was dedicated in 1893. Today the Lutheran congregation has around 350 members.

Above: Procession to the Grotto of the Nativity on Christmas Eve with the Latin patriarch of Jerusalem.

Left: The famous Midnight Mass in St. Catherine's Church on Christmas Eve.

The Syrian Orthodox Church has its roots in Greater Syria, Asia Minor, and Mesopotamia, going back to the fifth and sixth centuries. A permanent Syrian bishopric has had its seat in Jerusalem since 1471. It must have been around 1838 that the first Syrian Christians settled in Bethlehem. Most of the Syrian Christians came to Bethlehem at the beginning of this century as a result of the massacres in Turkey. The Church of St. Ephraim, named after the important Syrian theologian, was dedicated in 1935. Today the Syrian community, with about 1,000 members, is the third largest in Bethlehem.

In 1219/1220, St. Francis of Assisi visited the Holy Land. Following the Crusader era, the Franciscans have been present in the Holy Land ever since 1336. The initial nucleus for an indigenous Roman Catholic congregation in Bethlehem was established in 1550. The present Church of St. Catherine, built in 1880, was erected on the foundations of the Latin church of the Middle Ages. The Roman Catholic Church is the largest in Bethlehem with approximately 3,000 members.

The Grotto of St. Jerome below the northern apse of the Church of the Nativity. A tunnel leads from the grotto, containing an altar to St. Jerome, to the cell where the church father lived and worked.

بيت لحم ٢٠٠٠

Franciscan monk in the garden of St. Catherine's Church. The church was built between 1881 and 1888.

Right: Statue of St. Jerome in front of St. Catherine's Church. The death's head at the base of the monument symbolizes the saint's ascetic way of life and also human mortality.

Below: The cloister in the Monastery of St. Jerome dates back to the twelfth century. Of the original 64 double pillars only 20 remain.

The bell-tower of the Greek Orthodox monastery on the southeastern side of the Church of the Nativity. The conventual building dates from several different eras.

Page 51 above: Pillar relief at the entrance to the Milk Grotto. It shows Mary and Joseph on their flight to Egypt after the birth of Christ.

Page 51 below: Altar in the Milk Grotto. In 1494 the Franciscans built a monastery above the grotto. Today's chapel dates from 1872.

The Greek Catholic Church in Beit Sahour.

The Milk Grotto

Along the road south of the Church of the Nativity is a shrine called the Milk Grotto. This shrine is a demonstration of Catholic spirituality and popular religion from the Middle Ages.

According to tradition, while Mary and Joseph were fleeing Herod's soldiers on their way to Egypt they stopped in this cave for Mary to nurse the baby Jesus. A drop of milk fell upon the stone and it turned white. That is why many people continue to visit this site today.

In popular religion, many couples who have difficulty having children visit the shrine and take a small piece of white rock to place under their mattresses. Other women make vows in order to have a plenteous supply of milk for nursing.

Christmas in Bethlehem

No one exactly knows when Jesus was born. The Gospels do not give a date for the celebration of Christmas. Paul's letter to the Galatians only says that Christ was born "in the fullness of time". In a sense, Christmas is celebrated every day of the year as pilgrims make their own connections with this important event.

In the early history of Christianity a number of different dates were suggested for Jesus' birth, usually in the spring or fall. When Christianity was recognized under Constantine, however, more attention was given to the details of Jesus' life. At the same time as Helen was trying to establish the place of Jesus' birth, others recognized the importance of a common time to celebrate it. It was decided in Rome that the date of December 25 was quite appropriate because the Romans had previously celebrated the three-day festival of *Sol Invictus* in honor of the sun god during the time of the winter solstice. Since Jesus was referred to as the *Light of the World*, this substitution was quite natural. The first recorded celebration of Jesus' birth on December 25 took place in Rome in the year 338. This became the accepted date for saying the *Mass of Christ's* birth or *Christmas.*

Among Eastern Christians, however, January 6 became a more popular date. In the West, this was the date for Epiphany, or the coming of the Magi. The matter is a bit complicated because the Julian calendar did not allow extra days for leap years, so that the year no longer coincided with the seasons. A revised calendar, known as the Gregorian calendar, was adopted. Armenia, however, did not accept this revision and so its calendar was about twelve days different from that of the Orthodox Church. The celebration of Armenian Christmas is therefore on January 18.

That is why there are today three official celebrations of Christmas in Bethlehem: December 25 – Catholic and Protestant; January 6 – Orthodox; January 18 – Armenian.

On December 24, the Roman Catholic and Protestant churches celebrate Christmas Eve. The day begins at 11:00 a.m. when various dignitaries go to Rachel's Tomb to meet the Latin patriarch from Jerusalem. A long parade follows with various marching groups of scouts leading the patriarch to Manger Square. At 1:00

p.m., the official welcoming takes place in Manger Square with all the Franciscans and seminarians dressing in liturgical vestments and leaders of various churches accompanying the patriarch to the basilica.

The evening activities include choral songs and fireworks in Manger Square. The high point of the evening is the midnight Latin mass in St. Catherine's Church although smaller masses continue throughout the night in the Grotto of the Nativity.

Left: The brightly lit Church of the Nativity at Christmas.

Below: Political and ecclesiastical dignitaries accompany the Syrian Orthodox bishop to the Christmas celebration.

Page 54 and 55: Thousands of Palestinians, pilgrims and tourists gather at Manger Square on December 24. In 1995 Christmas celebrations took place for the first time after the retreat of the Israeli army.

Above: Christmas procession of Palestinian scouts in the city center of Bethlehem.

Right: Bagpipers of the Palestinian police in front of the Church of the Nativity with the bell-tower of the Armenian monastery in the background.

Chapter IV

Bethlehem and Its Surroundings

Beit Sahour

The modern village of Beit Sahour seems to have been established in the mid-thirteenth century, although it is not mentioned in Western literature until 1591. The ancient tradition seems to be preserved in the name *Beit Sahour*, meaning *the house of staying up all night,* which alludes to the tradition of shepherds keeping watch over their flocks at night. The sight of shepherds and flocks grazing on surrounding hillsides is still common today.

Because of the fertile soil in the valley, many residents turned to tenant farming for wealthy Bethlehemite landlords. In a sense, they also preserve another biblical tradition – of Ruth gleaning in the fields of Boaz, a story said to have taken place in this area.

Beit Sahour has the character of a large village with a structure based on extended families. It is somewhat closed in social terms so that there has been little of the immigration or emigration typical of nearby Bethlehem. The structure of the population, therefore, has remained fairly constant.

Beit Sahour is the town with the highest proportion of Christians in the area. The present population of about 11,000 residents includes 83 percent Christians. This is about the same ratio as the one recorded by the 1914 census. In the early nineteenth century there was probably a higher percentage of Muslims. However, many Muslims were drafted into the army of Ibrahim Pasha for the Egyptian rebellion against the Ottomans (1831-1839). Since then it has been primarily a Christian town.

The religions among residents of Beit Sahour are: Greek Orthodox 5,749, Latin Catholic 919, Greek Catholic 528, Protestant 105, Syrian Orthodox 44 and Muslim 1,650.

The Intifada in Beit Sahour

In recent years, Beit Sahour has also achieved a reputation as a center for creative non-violent resistance. During the Intifada, it was the only community to organize a tax boycott against occupying Israel. Under the slogans *No taxation under occupation* and *No taxation without representation,* its residents presented a clear challenge to Israel in a pamphlet that explained their position in the following words:

> We consider the occupation of one people by another people a clear violation of international law and religion. It is contrary to simple human rights and to democracy. The Israeli policy of collecting taxes contradicts international agreements, the Geneva and the Hague conventions in particular. In the 22 years of occupation, the Israeli authorities have not yet rendered an accounting of tax distribution in the West Bank.

Left: Springtime meadow south of Bethlehem.

View of Beit Sahour including the Greek Orthodox church and the mosque in the city center. During the Intifada, Beit Sahour was one of the strongholds of Palestinian resistance to the Israeli occupying forces. There are some important industrial plants here today.

The residents detailed the social programs not provided to their community including education, health, water, and electrical resources. They then concluded:

For these reasons – and as a consequence of our conviction that the money taken in by the high taxes we pay is spent on ammunition and tear gas used to kill our children – we have decided not to pay taxes anymore.

As a result, stiff penalties were assessed against the community. These included confiscation of property amounting to two million dollars, strict curfews, and house arrest for 40 days with even telephone lines cut and leaders imprisoned. Nevertheless, with local determination the city continued to flourish with a high number of privately financed social programs, hospitals, and rehabilitation centers. Education remains the highest priority, and Beit Sahour retains the distinction of having the highest percentage of college graduates among Palestinians.

Beit Sahour has also established the tradition of a Christmas night candlelight walk to symbolize its dedication to peace and justice. In recent years this has also included the participation of Israelis open to dialog. With the passing of Israeli occupation, the focus is now on the threat of land confiscation and the building of Jewish settlements in neighboring Abu Ghuneim (Har Homa).

بيت لحـم ٢٠٠٠

The Shepherds' Fields

In that region there were shepherds living in the fields, keeping watch over their flock by night (Luke 2:8).

With these words, Luke introduces the shepherds who saw the Christmas angels and then made their way to see the baby Jesus in the manger. This tradition has long been associated with the modern town of Beit Sahour, less than a mile east of Bethlehem.

According to Jerome, this was the site of *Migdal Eder* or the *Tower of the Flock*, where Jacob grazed his flock on his journey to Hebron following the death of Rachel (Genesis 35:21). The name was apparently associated with a region where there were watchtowers for shepherds to keep an eye on their grazing flocks.

Jerome observed these towers which continue to be characteristic of the Beit Sahour region. The *Mishnah* confirms that the sacrificial animals for the temple were grazed at Migdal Eder.

Later, the prophet Micah (4:8) alluded to this place when talking about the coming Messiah: "And you, O tower of the flock, hill of daughter of Zion, to you it shall come, the former dominion shall come, the sovereignty of daughter Jerusalem."

This theme was continued in the *Targums* – the Aramaic translations of the *Torah* – in Genesis 35:21. They identify the fields visited by Jacob with the place where the Messianic king would be revealed.

The Greek Orthodox Shepherds' Field with its church (built in 1972). The Catholic Shepherds' Field is situated about one kilometer northwest of this place.

Palestinian village between Beth-lehem and the Judean desert.

Thus it is not surprising that early Christian tradition assigned a particular location to the Christmas shepherds. From the reports of numerous pilgrims, it is clear that the name Shepherds' Field had become fixed, and their descriptions note an altar for prayer within a cave that was in turn set apart by a walled garden area. Later records also mention a Monastery of the Shepherds. By the fifth century, the old liturgies for Christmas included a vigil that took place on Christmas Eve before a procession moved to the Church of the Nativity in Bethlehem.

The literary traditions connected with the Shepherds' Field are somewhat complicated by the fact that archaeologists have uncovered several possible sites. On the north ridge of Beit Sahour is *Siyar el-Ghanam*, the place *for keeping sheep*. Here there is evidence for the occupation of various caves from the time of the New Testament as well as the remains of an ancient tower and olive presses. There are remains of a late fourth-century church and a sixth- to eighth-century monastery, which included a bakery, wine presses, and animal pens, as well as several mosaics with Greek inscriptions. Today this area is taken care of by the Franciscans. A modern church, built in 1954, is best known for the altar incorporating Palestinian sculpture.

A second site is known as *Kaniset el-Ruat*, the *Church of the Shepherds*. This site is located at the east end of the town at the modern Greek Orthodox church. Excavations have uncovered a fourth-century mosaic floor within a grotto over which was built a fifth-century church and then a larger sixth-century basilica. After this structure was destroyed in the Persian invasion of the early seventh century, a modest walled monastery was erected in its place which in turn was destroyed in the tenth century.

A third site is located at the YMCA Rehabilitation Center where there are a number of large caves. It has been designated as the Protestant Shepherds' Field.

The traditions connected with the Shepherds' Field pervade the entire area. The location of the controversial Israeli housing project *Har Homa* – across the modern political border in Greater Jerusalem – is still known by the Palestinians as *Abu Ghuneim*, which means *Place for Grazing*.

The ancient churches and monasteries connected with the Shepherds' Field were destroyed in the Middle Ages well before the Crusader period, and the entire area was abandoned for centuries. The tradition has been revived only in modern times.

Desert landscape east of Bethlehem. On the horizon, the Moab mountains in Jordan.

Herodium

The fortress, which is some 60 stades [12 kilometers] distant from Jerusalem, is naturally strong and very suitable for such a structure, for reasonably nearby is a hill, raised to a [greater] height by the hand of man and rounded off in the shape of a breast. At intervals it has round towers, and it has a steep ascent formed of 200 steps of hewn stone. Within it are costly royal apartments made for security and for ornament at the same time.

At the base of the hill there are pleasure grounds built in such a way as to be worth seeing, among other things because of the way in which water, which is lacking in that place, is brought in from a distance and at great expense. The surrounding plain has been built up as a city second to none, with the hill serving as an acropolis for the other dwellings.

So the ancient historian Josephus, in *Jewish Antiquities*, describes the fortress Herod built for himself around the year 20 B.C. Herod chose the site after an important military victory against the Hasmoneans of Jerusalem, which helped to launch his career in 40 B.C. As an Idumean, Herod was a descendant of Arab tribesmen, who originally lived both east of the Jordan River and in the southern part of Palestine, and thus was despised by the elite of Jerusalem. Because Herod liked this area very much, the palace was used for leisure during his lifetime; it also served as the family burial place and later, as his memorial.

Herod invested a great deal of labor and resources in various building projects, including the seaport of

Caesarea, the Jerusalem temple, the city of Sebaste (Samaria) near Nablus, and the Tomb of the Patriarchs in Hebron. Yet the Herodium is the enterprise he wished to be remembered for. He chose a natural hill of which he raised the level by vaults and then surrounded the structures on top with fill, so that the hill – rising 100 meters above its surroundings – is an imposing sight from Bethlehem five kilometers to the northwest.

The main structure consists of two parallel circular walls with a diameter of nearly 50 meters. Within this structure the eastern half was made up of a garden surrounded by columns. The western half included a triclinium dining room, a bath house, and dwelling quarters. 15 meters below floor level was a network of four plastered cisterns.

The remains at the bottom of the hill cover an expanse of 38 acres. Lower Herodium included a magnificent pool complex, a bathhouse, and other dwellings. The character of this place has been preserved in the Arabic name *Jebel Fureidis* or *Paradise Mountain.*

Just as Herod had designed this palace and burial place as a fortress, it was used in a military function by Jewish rebels in both the first (66-73) and second (132-135) revolts against Rome. These Zealots dug a network of security tunnels beneath the fortress, 300 meters of which have been explored.

After four centuries in which the Herodium appears to have been abandoned, the site began to be used as a religious center in the fifth century. On the top of the Herodium, one chapel appears to have been occupied by a monastic community.

Left: Remnants of pillars at the base of the Herodium, King Herod's palace structure, situated south-east of Bethlehem.

In the lower part of the Herodium, three different contemporary churches have been excavated, all having beautiful mosaic floors. Because the inscriptions vary from the usual forms expected in Greek Orthodox churches of this time, it has been suggested that this may have been a community belonging to a Gnostic sect. This theory is supported by the fact that the church is dedicated to the archangel Michael.

So this religious community stands in contrast to both the Greek Orthodox and Monophysite monasteries nearby. This community seems to have continued for several centuries into the early Arab period. These churches, once again, are evidence of pluralism within early Christianity and suggest an attitude of tolerance towards various expressions of faith within the region east of Bethlehem.

Tekoa

The Old Testament prophet Amos was from the village of Tekoa, south-east of Bethlehem. The name *Tekoa* probably means *the place for pitching tents*, which reflects its location on the eastern edge of the Judean hills where the wilderness begins. While the *Talmud* (the Jewish compendium of law and lore) noted the fertile area to the west covered with olive trees, the biblical writers often described the wilderness of Tekoa as a place of refuge during times of struggle (Jeremiah 6:1; 2 Chronicles 20:20).

According to biblical records, this city was founded by Ephrathites from Bethlehem in the north and by Calebites from Hebron in the south (1 Chronicles 2:24). It seems to have served as an administrative center in the kingdom of Judah and was also a fortified city (2 Chronicles 11:5). David apparently had connections with the residents of Tekoa and found support here (1 Chronicles 27:9).

When David had a falling out with his son Absalom, Joab made an attempt at reconciliation through the help of a wise woman from Tekoa (2 Samuel 14). Some have suggested, therefore, that Tekoa may have had a long tradition of wise and rhetorically skilled women leaders.

The eighth-century prophet Amos seems to have had relations to this tradition. As the prophet was called to speak out at the sanctuary Beth-El in the north, he noted his background as a herdsman and a tender of trees. He addressed moral wrong-doings, like self-indulgence, neglect of the poor, and religious complacency. His strong stand for social justice led to his deportation. Yet his message was so clear that he was the first prophet to have his words preserved in his own Old Testament book.

Today there are ruins from a memorial, presumably to Amos, dating back at least to the first century. This memorial consists of a double cave over which stood a square structure ten meters on a side. Nearby stand the ruins of a Byzantine St. Nicholas Church with mosaic floors, and a Monophysite monastery was also located here. The village continued to be important until at least the Crusader period. In more recent times the village has been relocated about two kilometers west of the ancient site. The Christian inhabitants of Tekoa migrated to Bethlehem in the eighteenth century. Today it is a Muslim village, which is well-known for its vegetables. Ironically, nearby there is also a modern Jewish settlement named Tekoa.

Left: Aerial view of the Herodium. The rounded shape of the mountain is clearly visible, due to the artificial raising of its level. The palace structure itself was originally framed by two parallel circular walls and four round towers. In the background is the Wadi Khureitun.

Solomon's Pools, engineered by King Herod, provided Jerusalem with water.

Solomon's Pools

Because Bethlehem is situated on the edge of the Judean desert, water is an important commodity. There are no natural springs, so residents have been dependent upon the rain which comes during the winter season from November to March and which is collected in cisterns. The fruitfulness of Bethlehem has therefore always been viewed by Bethlehemites as a gift from God.

It has also been common for Bethlehemites to dig deep wells to provide water. The biblical 2 Samuel 23:1-17 records the story of David who was camped nearby Bethlehem at a time when it was held as a Philistine garrison. David looked to the town of Bethlehem and exclaimed: "O that someone would give me water to drink from the well of Bethlehem that is by the gate!" Although three soldiers broke through enemy lines to bring David a drink of water, he poured it out upon the ground. David knew that water should not be squandered, causing a threat to existence, but that it was God's gift of life, to be shared equally by all. Today along the road leading out of Bethlehem, visitors are often shown three rock cisterns known as David's Wells.

Solomon's Pools, located about four kilometers south of Bethlehem, have played a significant role in the area's water supply for centuries. The three pools are each over 100 meters long and ten meters deep and have a combined capacity of nearly 300,000 cubic meters of water.

These pools are fed by four different springs, the most prominent with the name Ein-Atan or Etam. It is named as one of the fortifications of Judah, underscoring its importance in biblical times. According to the first-century Jewish historian Josephus, this was one of Solomon's favorite places: "Now there was a certain spot eight miles distant from Jerusalem which is called Etam, delightful for, and abounding in, parks and flowing streams, and to this place he would make excursions, mounted high on his chariot."

The present pools were probably constructed by Herod the Great in connection with his improvements to the Jerusalem temple. Yet the name of Solomon continued to be associated with them, probably because of Ecclesiastes 2:5-6, which reads: "I made myself gardens and parks, and planted in them all kinds of fruit trees. I made myself pools from which to water the forest of growing trees."

The area around Solomon's Pools has provided a pleasant atmosphere for picnics and relaxation over the centuries. On the north side at the entry to the park is an old structure, built in 1620, which is known as *Qalat el-Burak* or the *castle of the pools*. This has served at times as a *khan* (a resting place for caravans) and a restaurant with a garden area inside.

The water system as a whole shows a high degree of sophistication. Five different aqueducts, totaling nearly 60 kilometers in length, were linked to Solomon's Pools. Two of them connected additional water sources from the south; another carried water east to the Herodium where Herod had constructed a lovely large recreational pool, lined with columns; and two aqueducts brought water to Jerusalem.

Josephus mentions one of the aqueducts in connection with the public works of Pontius Pilate. The *Talmud* also describes Ein-Atan as the source for water at the temple and mentions that the flow of water was possible because of the difference in elevation. The *Talmud* also mentions that in 70 Jewish Zealots destroyed the aqueduct which passed through Bethlehem. The tenth Roman legion was responsible for rebuilding the last of these aqueducts, the one following the present Jerusalem-Hebron road. This section of it contains some 24 inscriptions with names of Roman soldiers including Julius Clemens, known to be a Roman consul in 195. Other remaining portions of the aqueduct can be seen at various places including sections along Hebron Road and Caritas Street.

A portion of the early aqueduct ran underneath the town of Bethlehem through a 400-meter-long tunnel. This remained a source of water for Bethlehem for nearly 2,000 years. After various stages of repairs under the Ottomans it went out of use when the British installed iron pipes and pumping stations. In recent times, residents of Bethlehem have relied on their own wells as a source of water. These beautiful wells can be seen in many courtyards of the older houses.

Page 70: The nunnery Hortus Conclusus (closed garden) in Artas, south of Bethlehem. The Archbishop of Montevideo had it built in 1901. According to tradition, Solomon's gardens were situated in Artas, a valley with rich vegetation.

Beit Jala

To the west of Bethlehem is situated the city of Beit Jala. This town of about 12,000 inhabitants covers the eastern slopes of Ras Jala, one of the highest mountains (923 meters above sea level) in the Judean Hills.

The name *Jala* means *Carpet of Grass* and probably refers to the pleasant appearance of this mountain. Some have seen a connection with biblical Giloh, which is mentioned among the cities of Judah in Joshua 15:51. Others, however, locate that city further to the south because of 2 Samuel 15:12. Yet others suggest that this may once have been the biblical city of Gallim mentioned by Isaiah 10:30 in connection with the eighth-century B.C. Assyrian invasion.

Because of the presence of the historic spring Bir Onah, it is likely that this was the site of an ancient settlement. However, no archaeological excavations have explored this town. Tradition says that in the eighth century B.C., the Assyrian army under Sennacherib camped here while besieging Jerusalem. According to 2 Kings 19:35, the army suffered a plague and the city of Jerusalem was spared.

There was a Christian village located here in the Middle Ages that fought against the Crusaders and was destroyed. It seems to have been abandoned until the eighteenth century.

The modern town of Beit Jala was established in the eighteenth century by Christian tribes from Wadi Musa in Jordan. In the early nineteenth century, the inhabitants were punished severely when they offered refuge to Muslims from Hebron who resisted the rebellion of the Egyptian Ibrahim Pasha. In 1907, when the Ottomans began drafting for their army, a high proportion of residents began emigrating to South America. Following the war of 1948, many Muslims from the south-west part of Jerusalem were forced to emigrate to Beit Jala.

Like Beit Sahour, Beit Jala is structured like a closed village; the population mainly consists of many extended families. 70 percent of Beit Jala's residents today are Christians.

In the nineteenth century Beit Jala was also home to a very important Russian Orthodox school, which has now become the Iskander Khoury Public School, named after the renowned writer. The Protestant Talitha Kumi School is one of the best in the West Bank. Today Beit Jala also hosts many important rehabilitation centers.

Because of its higher altitude and cooler temperatures, Beit Jala is attractive as a summer resort. Residents of other Arab countries have established their summer homes there. In 1847, Giuseppe Valerga, the first Latin patriarch, chose Beit Jala for his summer residence. This building was later converted into the Latin seminary where nearly all Arab Catholic priests, including

Terraced fruit-tree and vineyards near Beit Jala.

present patriarch Michael Sabbah, received their training. On the northern slopes of Ras Jala is located the Salesian Cremisan Monastery with its famous winery.

Iskander Khoury

One of the most important twentieth-century Palestinian writers is Iskander Khoury. He was born in 1890, the son of an Orthodox priest in Ein Kerem, and he spent most of his childhood in Beit Jala where he was sent to be educated. He studied theology, Arabic, and law in Cairo and Beirut as well as in Bethlehem and Nazareth. He settled in the area first as a teacher in Beit Jala, then as a judge in Bethlehem and later in Jerusalem, where he died in 1973.

Throughout his life, Iskander Khoury wrote articles, short stories, and poetry. He was influenced by the Arab nationalist movement and a concern for the rights of women. He wrote extensively following the disaster of 1948 known as al-Nakba.

In 1935, on the occasion of feuding in Haifa between a Christian family and a Muslim family, he wrote the following poem with the title "Christians are the Brothers of the Muslims":

"Know the hand of conspiracy will not destroy The unity of the two religions. We were and we still are as we were Serving this homeland. Before Christ and before Muhammad We were and we still are Arabs. We had and we still have our homeland As mother and father. And no religion unites us, but the religion of Love and family relationships."

Rachel's Tomb

Near the entrance to Bethlehem, just west of Hebron road, is a structure known since the Middle Ages as Rachel's Tomb. This is first attested to by the Bordeaux Pilgrim, who made a visit in 333 and wrote: "Four miles from Jerusalem, on the right of the highway to Bethlehem, is the tomb in which was laid Jacob's wife Rachel."

The historicity of the site is questionable. The commemoration of Rachel here may be due to a confusion of names. Jerome identified the tomb by the Hebron road as commemorating Herod's son Archelaus, who ruled Judea. It is not difficult to see how confusion could arise between the names *Rachel* and *Archelaus* – especially by someone just passing through.

بيت لحم ٢٠٠٠

Left: Rachel's Tomb is an important place to pray for pious Jews. Muslims and Christians also venerate the tomb.

Rachel's Tomb north of Bethlehem by the road from Jerusalem to Hebron. In 1998 it has been surrounded by a high wall.

Genesis 35:19 reports that Rachel died giving birth to Benjamin while she and Jacob were traveling from Beth-El to Hebron and that a pillar was erected in memory of her on the way to Ephrath – that is, Bethlehem. While Genesis would seem to point to the modern commemorative tomb, the description is really rather vague. A contrary view is presented in 1 Samuel 10:2 – namely that Rachel's Tomb is located north of Jerusalem in the territory of Benjamin near Er-Ram. In this place, residents of Jerusalem were gathered before being deported to Babylon in the sixth century B.C. so that Jeremiah 31:15 lamented: "A voice is heard in Ramah, lamentation and bitter weeping. Rachel is weeping for her children; she refuses to be comforted because they are no more."

Later, when Matthew recounted the story of the slaughter of young boys from Bethlehem by King Herod, he recalled Jeremiah's words.

From the time of the Middle Ages the tomb has been venerated by Muslims, Jews, and Christians. The present structure, within a Muslim cemetery, is the result of construction activities by Crusaders in the thirteenth century, Muhammad Pasha of Jerusalem in the sixteenth century, and Moses Montefiore in the nineteenth century. Such cooperation is especially appropriate considering the role of Rachel as a matriarch respected in all three monotheistic religions.

The Church of the Kathisma

Early Christians recognized the difficulty of women traveling during their pregnancy. North of the Bethlehem checkpoint near the Mar Elias Monastery was located a shrine commemorating the resting place of Mary and Joseph on the way to Jerusalem. The focal point was a six-foot-wide rock where Mary sat.

Pilgrims began to frequent the location as early as the third century. The later fifth-century octagonal structure, measuring 58 by 48 meters, was once the largest octagonal church in the Holy Land. Green and yellow mosaic floors present geometric designs as well as palm leaves and dates. The commemorative octagonal church was destroyed in the ninth century and its remnants were only recently discovered by construction workers. Today it is again covered in earth.

Below: The Judean desert near the Mar Saba Monastery.

Right: Village near Bethlehem.

بيت لحـــم ٢٠٠٠

CHAPTER V

Monasteries around Bethlehem

Monasteries

Over 100 monasteries flourished in the Judean desert to the east of Bethlehem during the fourth through sixth centuries. After founding the first monastery in the Jordan Valley, Chariton, known as the founder of Palestinian monasticism, also established the monastery at Souka, three kilometers from Tekoa. The monastic movement became quite successful so that the desert bloomed with monasteries, where monks sometimes shared their whole life together (*coenobia* system) and in other cases gathered only for a weekly Eucharist after living separate lives in surrounding caves (*laura* system). While this important movement began to decline with the Persian invasion, a number of these monasteries, including Theodosius and Mar Saba, are still active today.

The monastic movement began for a number of reasons. One has to do with pilgrimage. Many monks began as pilgrims who followed in the footsteps of Christ, first visiting Bethlehem and Jerusalem and then going out into the wilderness for 40 days to struggle with temptation. Also, with the acceptance of Christianity under Constantine, many who knew the struggles of the Christians during persecutions now felt that the Christian life had become too easy and that faith was often taken for granted.

Some, therefore, saw the idea of going to the desert to be the highest of virtues. There it was thought that they could be away from the world and closer to God.

Left: The Greek Orthodox Mar Saba Monastery, in the almost vertical rockface of Wadi Kidron, is one of the oldest monasteries in the world. Its architecture, significance in terms of religious history and fantastic situation in the desert make a visit an unforgettable experience.

Chronology of Holy Land Monasticism

308	*Hilarion begins life as hermit near Gaza*
330	*Chariton establishes Pharan Monastery near Jericho*
350	*Chariton establishes Souka Monastery near Tekoa and Hanging Cave*
476	*Theodosius Monastery established*
478	*Sabas begins life as hermit in cave*
483	*Sabas establishes the Great Laura in Wadi Kidron*
532	*Sabas dies and is buried at Mar Saba*
560	*Cyril of Scythopolis writes "The Lives of the Monks of Palestine"*
580	*"Life of Chariton"*
726	*John of Damascus writes in defense of icons at Mar Saba*
877	*"Summa Theologiae Arabica" written in Mar Saba*

In doing so, they also felt that they were fulfilling prophecy by making the desert bloom, with places of prayer dotting the landscape.

Monastic life in Palestine was paradoxical by nature. Although the monks retreated to the desert, the monasteries were positioned in Wadi Kidron and Wadi Khureitun, where there was an abundance of water and the necessities of life were available. Although monasticism appears to be a retreat from the world, the monks still remained very much involved in the concerns of society. Many people viewed the monks as

بيت لحــم ٢٠٠٠

holy men and sought them out for advice and intercessory prayer.

Monks from the Holy Land participated in the theological discussions of the great ecumenical councils. During the Christological debate following the Council of Chalcedon in 451, Sabas and other monks took a leading role in opposing the Monophysites of Jerusalem, who rejected the two natures of Christ.

The Life of Sabas

Sabas was born in Cappadocia in the year 439 and began the monastic life at the age of eight. When he was 18 he left for Palestine and joined the monks Euthymius and Theoctistus. After journeying into the desert area south-east of Jerusalem to fast each Lent, nourishing himself only with the bread and wine of the Eucharist, he chose in 478 to take up the life of a hermit in an isolated cave in the Wadi Kidron. Within five years, 70 others had joined him in neighboring caves among the cliffs. Sabas structured their daily lives around solitary prayer, seven times a day, and work, such as basket weaving. Sabas established the Great Laura where the monks came from their isolated cells once a week to join in community for Eucharist and to obtain supplies necessary for the coming week. When the number of followers grew to 150, Sabas set out to establish nine additional monasteries. He died in 532. In the twelfth century his body was carried off to Venice by crusaders, but it was returned to Mar Saba Monastery in 1965 at the time of the papal visit to Palestine. Sabas was given the Aramaic title *Mar*, which means *Saint*.

Following the Arab conquest in the seventh century, the monks gathered permanently within the protective walls of the compound. Since that time, Mar Saba Monastery has been established as a *coenobia*, where monks share a communal life of work, prayers, and common meals. The complex centers on the Theotokos Church in honor of Mary and the Church of St. Nicholas, which surround the central courtyard where the tomb of St. Sabas is located. Four additional chapels provide for daily prayer. In addition to rooms for individual monks, there is a communal dining room, kitchen, bakery, and hospital. No less than 20 cisterns can be found within the monastery. There is a hospice for pilgrims. However, no female visitors have ever been admitted. The neighboring women's tower is provided for women who wish to make a pilgrimage.

The Mar Saba Monastery remains active in the modern era. At the end of a long, winding road, it is the culmination for many pilgrims, and it provides a base point for the hearty few wishing to venture on foot among the ancient caves of the Wadi Kidron.

The Mar Saba Monastery and Wadi Kidron in a drawing by Charles Wilson (1865).

بيت لحـــم ٢٠٠٠

The Monasteries and the Local Arab Population

From 532 to the twelfth century the chapel in the monastery's court-yard served as a tomb for St. Sabas. Since 1965 his bones have rested in the main church of the monastery. Today only about a dozen monks still live in Mar Saba; in the sixth century there were at times about 5,000.

There are a number of stories which speak of conflict between the monasteries and the local population. Indeed, 20 monks from Mar Saba were martyred in 797. But many positive episodes emphasize that the lives of foreign monks and the local population were closely intertwined.

In the early fourth century, an Arab sheik sought out the monk Euthymius to heal his paralyzed son. As a commander of horsemen under the Persians, he had sought out help among various magi, but to no avail. A dream of his son directed him to a grey-haired bearded monk who lived in a gorge south of the Jerusalem-Jericho road. The boy recognized Euthymius from his dream and was healed by him. The sheik and his tribe were then baptized and his brother-in-law Maris remained to become a monk and eventually the head of the Theoctistus Monastery.

At many monasteries, there have also been examples of the local population regularly leaving generous gifts of food and supplies for the monks. The Theodosius Monastery to the east of Bethlehem has had a history of positive interaction with the surrounding people. Theodosius selected the site because tradition said that the wise men had stayed in this cave while fleeing from Herod. Yet only on discovering an anonymous gift was he actually able to construct the large monastery. He included a hospital, a home for the elderly, and a dining room to provide as many as 100 tables set for the poor. The local Arab name for the monastery, fittingly, was *Ibn Abeid,* which means *Son of the Humble Servant.*

The Theodosius Monastery became one of the largest in the area with over 400 monks. At the request of Sabas, hundreds of workers came from Asia Minor to assist in its work, and their descendants continued to serve the monastery until the middle of the nineteenth century. After the Arab conquest in the seventh century, these Greek Christian servants were Arabized in language and culture, and in the fourteenth century they became Muslims. After centuries of semi-Bedouin life, they settled in the village surrounding the monastery, which then took the name *Abeidiya,* meaning the *Place of the Servant.*

ΤΟΙΣ ΫΜΑΣ ΧΡΕΟΣ ΑΝΤΕΣ ΑΥΤΟΣ ΩΣ ΡΟΔΑ ΟΙΚΗΤΕ ΠΑΡΑΔΕΙΣΟΝ ΑΝΕΡΕΣ ΘΕΟΙ ΕΝ ΤΗ ΛΑΥΡΑ ΤΟΥ ΠΡΣ ΣΑΒΒΑ
ΟΛΕΣΘΕ ΛΟΙΠΟΝ ΤΗΣ ΫΜΑΣ ΖΩΓΡΑΦΕΙ ΒΗΣΣΑΡΙΩΝΙ Κ ΙΩΑΝΝΙΚΙΩ ΟΙ ΜΕΝ ΕΝ ΕΤΕΙ ΑΠΟ ΧΫ ΧΙΕ ΔΙΑ ΧΟΣΡΟΫ
ΕΚΔΟΦΥΛΑΞΙ ΤΟΥ ΠΑΝΑΓΙΟΥ ΤΑΦΟΥ ΑΦΙΕΡΩΣΕΙΤ ΕΝΘΑ ΑΠΕΚΤΑΝΘΗΤΕ ΟΙΔΕ ΕΝ ΤΩ ͵ΑΩΑ ΔΙΑ ΑΡΕΩΝ
ΙΣΤΟΡΙΘΗ ΕΝ ΕΤΕΙ ͵ΑΩΓ ΗΜΕΝ ΔΙΟΝΤΟΣ ΞΕΝΙΚΗ ΠΑ ΘΕΜ ΗΜΑ Ο

John of Damascus

Following the emergence and expansion of Islam, many Christians continued to play vital roles as government technocrats. John of Damascus, born in 675, was the son of one of these officials, Sargun Ibn Mansour, finance minister and director of Christian affairs of the Islamic state in Damascus. John was trained to follow in his father's footsteps in government work, but later chose the monastic life instead. He came to Palestine in 716 where he was installed as a bishop in the church by the patriarch of Jerusalem. He joined the Mar Saba Monastery, where he became one of the world's most important theologians. His greatest work was called *The Fountain of Knowledge*. The primary focus of his writings was the defense of Christianity in its encounter with Islam.

During the iconoclastic controversy, John of Damascus played a crucial role. Muslim belief, of course, forbade the use of images. Yet it was the Byzantine emperor Leo III who declared images idolatrous for Christians. While theologians within the empire were silenced by threat of persecution, it was John, living under the protection of Mar Saba Monastery, who had sufficient freedom to argue that icons were important in the Christian faith. His argument has been preserved as follows:

Page 80-83: The collection of icons at the Mar Saba Monastery is one of the most famous in the world. During the iconoclastic controversy (726-843) many icons were brought to safety at Mar Saba.

Page 80: The birth of Christ.

Page 81: The Persians attack the Mar Saba Monastery in 614.

Page 82: Saints and church fathers.

Page 83: John of Damascus. From Mar Saba he became the most important advocate of the veneration of icons.

We use all our senses to produce worthy images of God, and we sanctify the noblest of the senses, which is that of sight. For just as words edify the ear, so also the image stimulates the eye. What the book is to the literate, the image is to the illiterate. Just as words speak to the ear, so the image speaks to the sight; it brings us understanding.

John's theological writings concerning icons were given official sanction by the Seventh Ecumenical Council at Nicea in 787.

When Christian iconoclasts began destroying icons, many of the oldest of them were rescued and preserved at Mar Saba, as well as at St. Catherine's Monastery in the Sinai. John of Damascus himself is one of the few saints portrayed in traditional Arabic dress on icons.

The Arabization of Theology

The monasteries in the Bethlehem region were centers for the Arabization of theology. With the Muslim conquest in 638, Arabic became the common language of the Holy Land, and Islam became the predominant religion. Greek-speaking theologians, such as John of Damascus, continued to dominate the scene for about a century. However, when the Ummayads of Damascus were replaced in power by the Abbasids of Baghdad, the result was a more confrontational attitude between Islam and Christianity. This political shift brought an end to the era of Greek-speaking monks who had close connections with Constantinople. The church in the Holy Land was in a sense severed from the rest of Christendom. In many Western history books, there is a gap in the story of Palestinian Christianity at this point. However, the monasteries continued to flourish.

It has been suggested that there was something of a school of Arab theology which had its center in the monasteries of Mar Saba and Chariton from 750 to 1050. Western as well as Arab scholars are only now beginning to recognize the wealth of material in the Arabic Christian manuscripts composed during this period. Many such literary resources are held at Mar Saba. Likewise, the library of St. Catherine's Monastery in the Sinai possesses numerous manuscripts which note these two monasteries as the place of composition and which list the names of the monks involved. Among the leading theologians were monks such as Theodore Abu Qurrah, who came from Edessa; Stephen from Ramlah; and Anthony David from Baghdad. However, the most important theological work from this era is the anonymous *Summa Theologiae Arabica* composed in 877.

Not only was the language used in the monasteries predominantly Arabic, but the main focus of theology was the dialog between Christians and Muslims. It was thus a contextual theology, which was quite foreign to both Latin and Orthodox branches of the church. Yet in the Holy Land it was dynamic and vital. While Rome and Constantinople were splitting further apart in theology and practice, Palestinian Christianity was characterized by an ecumenical spirit for the sake of a unified response to Islam.

Revival of Monastic Movements

Although monasticism flourished in the fourth through sixth centuries and has continued through the present, there has been a resurgence in the modern era. Thus there is once again a flourishing of monasteries throughout the area. While the earlier movement was more Eastern in character, this nineteenth- and twentieth-century monastic revival is mostly Western. Today these orders are involved in education, health, social and economic development as well as the spiritual life.

The Work of Modern Orders in Bethlehem

1333	Franciscans	education, guest house, custody of holy sites
1848	Sisters of St. Joseph	education
1873	Sisters of Mercy	women's work
1875	Carmelite Sisters	contemplative life
1876	Brothers of Christian Schools	education
1880	Rosary Sisters	education
1885	Franciscans – Coeur Immaculé de Marie	kindergarten, handicrafts
1886	Sisters of Charity St. Vincent de Paul	hospital
1891	Salesians	vocational training, winery
1901	Sisters of Hortus Conclusus	orphanage
1909	White Sisters (Franciscans de Marie)	early childhood education, family education, counseling
1927	Sisters of San Dorothea	rehabilitation for persons with hearing and speech disorders
1949	Small Sisters of Jesus	handicrafts
1958	Salvatoriennes	education
1972	Benedictine Sisters	handicrafts
1974	Sisters of the Apostles/Sisters of Doronea	dormitory for students, care for mentally impaired children
1985	Maronite Sharbel House	guest house

Crosses on lintels over doors in Bethlehem.

The Rosary Sisters

The Rosary Sisters were established in 1880 by Father Yusef Tannous from Nazareth and Sister Mary Alphonsene, previously of St. Joseph's Order in Bethlehem. Both agreed that there was a need for an order composed only of Arab nuns. In 1893, the first five Arab nuns came to Bethlehem, teaching young women sewing. Today the Rosary Sisters have established a reputation for excellent schools and are the largest order serving in the Holy Land. In addition, they have expanded so that they now serve in Palestine, Israel, Jordan, Lebanon, the Gulf States, and Rome. They were officially recognized as an order of the Roman Catholic Church by papal decree on 4 August 1959.

Abu Ghuneim

On the road to Jerusalem, the Mar Elias Monastery was established in the fifth century to commemorate the flight of the Old Testament prophet Elijah from Queen Jezebel to the desert. Nearby, a number of other monasteries from the fifth century, as well as the newly discovered Church of Kathisma, were built on the beautiful forested hill called *Abu Ghuneim*.

Prior to 1967, political boundaries mirrored the connection of this area with Bethlehem. In fact, the name *Abu Ghuneim*, literally meaning *Place for Grazing*, reflects the historical connections with shepherds from Bethlehem and Beit Sahour. However, modern political boundaries have included the hillside within the greater Jerusalem municipality so that the military checkpoint has been located just to the south of the hill. Because of the religious, environmental, and historic importance of *Abu Ghuneim*, plans for the Israeli *Har Homa* housing development have been extremely controversial.

Window in St. Catherine's Church.

Left: View of Bethlehem with the Lutheran Christmas Church and the Church of the Nativity in the center.

City Panoramas

Above: View of Bethlehem from Beit Sahour.

Below: View of Bethlehem's city center with the Mosque of Omar, Manger Square and the Church of the Nativity.

The Historic Quarters of Bethlehem

The modern city of Bethlehem began to develop during the Middle Ages as various tribal groups settled in particular quarters. Houses commonly opened toward a central courtyard where business and government matters were discussed and where the social life of the community was enjoyed. Such community organization made it possible for the members of each quarter to retain their distinctive identity while being part of the same city.

Two Christian tribal groups came to Bethlehem along with Caliph Omar Ibn al-Khattab from the Arabian peninsula in the early seventh century. Today they constitute the two largest family groups in the modern city of Bethlehem.

The residents of Najajarah to the west of Manger Square came from Najran in Yemen. They include a sub-group called Gathabreh, which had earlier come to Bethlehem from Greece and was then incorporated into the Najajarah quarter. The residents of Farahiyah, to the northwest of Manger Square along the ancient Star Street, are named after their patriarch Farah from Wadi Musa in Jordan.

With the coming of the Crusaders, a third quarter was established directly north of Manger Square called Tarajmah. This name is related to the role of its residents as translators and guides for pilgrims.

بيت لحــم ٢٠٠٠

Three additional Christian tribes settled in Bethlehem during the Ottoman period. The residents of Antarah, to the south of the Church of the Nativity, came from the village of Antar near the Herodium. The residents of Qawawseh, to the south of Manger Square, came from Tekoa. The residents of Hraizat, to the north of Manger Square near the new road, came from Um Tuba south of Jerusalem.

The first Muslim quarter was also established during the Ottoman period. The residents of Fawagrah, on the hill to the west of the city center, came from the village of Fagur near Solomon's Pools.

The eighth and last quarter was established only in the twentieth century. This is the Syrian quarter, which is just north of the steps of the market in Star square. This group is distinctive because its origins are in the area of Syria near Turkey where the people speak Aramaic, the spoken language of the New Testament era. Several families settled in Bethlehem in the mid-nineteenth century, but greater numbers arrived after the early twentieth-century massacres in Turkey.

Even today many of the houses of natural white stone open toward a central courtyard. Apart from traditional architecture which is marked by narrow alleys and various arches, modern styles have also developed since the beginning of the twentieth century. They were partly influenced by former emigrants to America, Europe and the Gulf States who have returned home.

Faces of a City

Farmer woman from El-Khader.

Left: Old man with a quffiye, the traditional Palestinian head scarf. The square cloth is held in place by a double head-ring (iqal) of a black cord of twisted camel or goat hair.

Page 94-97: Scenes from everyday life.

Today the Bethlehem district consists of the three towns Bethlehem, Beit Sahour and Beit Jala and about 70 villages. Of the 140,000 Palestinians living in this area 67 percent are Muslims and 33 percent Christians.

Palestinian woman from Bethlehem.

بيت لحـم ٢٠٠٠

CHAPTER VI

Bethlehem: Christian-Muslim Coexistence

Islam in Bethlehem

The Muslim calendar begins in 622 when Muhammad migrated from Mecca to Medina and established the Muslim community. It was during the years following the prophet's death that Islam spread to the Holy Land under the leadership of the second Caliph Omar Ibn al-Khattab.

Bethlehem is an important place for Muslims. Because Jesus (Isa) is recognized as a prophet in Islam and because the story of the Virgin Miriam and the birth of Jesus is included in the Quran, Christmas and the Church of the Nativity are assigned great significance by Muslims.

From the earliest time, the stage was set for a positive attitude of mutual toleration between Christians and Muslims. When the Caliph Omar first visited Bethlehem in 637 and it was the time for prayer, the Christian patriarch Sophronius invited him to say his prayers in the south apse of the Church of the Nativity. From that point on it became customary for Muslims to pray in that part of the church, and out of respect for the belief of the Muslims that forbids religious images the Christians removed all images from the south apse.

According to tradition, the Caliph Omar responded by issuing an edict which promised safety to Christians and respect for their worship and shrines.

Left: Artfully intertwined Arabic characters are typical of Islamic art. The calligraphic cross of Adel Nasser reflects the influence of this art form on the work of Christian painters. The calligraphic text reads: "Glory to God in the highest heaven, and peace on earth to those with whom he is pleased" (Luke 2:14).

Muslims in Bethlehem

For most of the last 2,000 years, Bethlehem has been associated closely with Christianity. The first Muslims who settled in Bethlehem in the mid-eighteenth century were from the village of Fagour south-west of Solomon's Pools. Originally they migrated to the Holy Land at the time of Salah ed-Din (twelfth century) from Turkey and Kurdistan. During Ottoman rule, the people of the village of Fagour came to the aid of Bethlehemites against a certain Arab sheik who had been antagonistic towards them. As a result, they were invited to settle in the south-west section of Bethlehem on the prominent hill which today makes up the city center. This is therefore known as the *Fawagreh District*.

With the Muslim population restricted mostly to one of the eight districts in Bethlehem, it still remained a small minority in the 1933 British census. Then 420 Muslims resided in Bethlehem out of a total population of 6,195, or less than seven percent. The situation began to change following the 1948 war with Israel when three refugee camps were established in Bethlehem. Since 1980, further immigration to Bethlehem has occurred mainly for economic reasons, with residents from Hebron and the semi-Bedouin Taamrah tribe from north-east of Bethlehem making up the greatest numbers. Today Muslims make up 59 percent of the population of Bethlehem.

To give an example of Christian-Muslim cooperation, representation of the Bethlehem district in the Palestinian National Authority is divided equally among Christians and Muslims.

Religious pluralism is also reflected in the work of the Al-Liqa Center. It was established in order to promote dialog between various Christian groups as well as personal contacts between Christians, Muslims and Jews.

Letter of Caliph Omar (637)

I implore the Almighty God for honoring us with Islam, dignifying our souls with the taste of faith, bestowing mercy upon us through our Muslim Prophet Muhammad (May peace be upon him), guiding us to the right way after being indulged in backwardness and ignorance, uniting our efforts from a state of loss and disunity, intimating between our hearts, helping us in conquering our enemy and enabling us to rule these vast areas of lands and peoples. Oh believers in God, thank Him for this gift.

This is Omar Ibn al-Khattab's letter to the dignified Patriarch Sophronius of Elijah's city on the Mount of Olives. It is a pledge to grant peace and safety for all Christians and clergymen and women wherever they are and at any place they wish to move and settle over our land.

Their churches, houses, shrines, and properties are secured inside and outside Jerusalem. The power of Patriarch Sophronius will extend in addition to the Church of the Holy Sepulchre in Jerusalem and the Church of the Nativity in Bethlehem with its three gates, the eastern, northern, and southern, to all other Christian races residing there including the Iberians, Ethiopians, Coptic, Syrian, Armenian, Nestorians, Jacobites, and Maronite pilgrims.

Our Prophet Muhammad ordered us to render good treatment to all believers in God including Christians and Jews. In following the teachings of Islam and the Sunna of our Prophet, the Caliph Omar is exempting Christians from the taxes of Kharaj and Gaffer imposed at that time, and from any other taxes on land or on sea. They must be treated cordially and given the freedom to perform their religious rites at the Church of the Sepulchre. All pilgrims visiting the Christian shrines are required to pay a fee of one and a half durham of silver to the patriarch.

All Muslims must abide by the spirit of this accord whether they be a sultan, a judge, rich or poor, man or woman.

This is drafted in the presence of the first vanguards of Islam, the companions of our prophet Abdullah, Othman Ibn Affan, Saad Ibn Zeid, and Abdel Rahman Ibn Auf. Any person coming after me should hand this accord to his successor to follow accordingly.

This document was written on 20 Rabi Awal 15 Hijra year.

Any person who may impeach the rulings of this document will be an enemy of God and his beloved Prophet Muhammad from now until the day of judgment.

Left: The Mosque of Omar with its slender minaret in the city center of Bethlehem. From there the muezzin calls the Muslims to prayer.

Page 102 and 103: Muslims at prayer. The highest Islamic duty is to perform the ritual prayer (salat) five times a day. It is closely connected with certain conditions and times: after the first sura of the Quran has been recited in a standing position, the suguda follows, which means that the palms of both hands, knees and the tips of the toes touch the ground. According to Islamic belief the prayer can be performed anywhere, preferably in a mosque. While praying the believers face the direction of Mecca.

بيت لحم ٢٠٠٠

Christian-Muslim Population among Palestinians

Christians	Location	Muslims
7 %	World-wide	93 %
3 %	Gaza and West Bank	97 %
27 %	Bethlehem District	73 %
41 %	Bethlehem City	59 %
70 %	Beit Jala	30 %
83 %	Beit Sahour	17 %
13 %	Arabs in Israel (plus 10 percent Druze)	77 %

The most important mosque for Muslims in Bethlehem is the Mosque of Omar on the west side of Manger Square. Originally a Byzantine church dedicated to John the Evangelist stood in this spot. In 1861, this church was donated by the Orthodox patriarch to the Muslim community for use as a mosque. The present mosque was built in 1954.

Pilgrimage in Islam

One of the pillars of Islam is the great pilgrimage to Mecca known as the *Hajj*. All Muslims are expected to take part in the Hajj sometime in their lifetime. So when the believers pray five times a day, they do so while facing in the direction of the city of Mecca.

Jerusalem is considered the third holiest site in Islam, and it is considered very important to pray at the Dome of the Rock. Many people therefore make pilgrimage to Jerusalem, then continuing to Hebron, where the tombs of the patriarchs are located. Bethlehem and the Church of the Nativity are also natural stopping points for these pilgrims because of their connection to Jesus' birth.

Sharing a Saint: El-Khader

In the popular religion of Palestine, the figure of El-Khader plays a prominent role. His story has roots going back to the Syrian and Babylonian fertility gods Adonis and Tammuz as well as to the "Epic of Gilgamesh" and the "Romance of Alexander the Great". He is seen as a figure who seeks the fountain of eternal youth. He is associated with the Old Testament prophet Elijah and St. George in the Christian tradition. However, the name El-Khader comes from the Quran. Because he is a figure who never dies, he appears in numerous forms and places throughout Palestine.

The name "El-Khader" literally means "The Green", which makes this figure especially appropriate in the Bethlehem region because of El-Khader's association with fertility. Many couples who have difficulty conceiving children seek his help and later dedicate their children to him. Others seek his help with illnesses.

South of Bethlehem is the village of El-Khader where there is a Greek Orthodox church dedicated to St. George. Both Muslims and Christians visit this shrine on a regular basis. At the entrance to the village is a stone relief showing the figure of St. George mounted on a horse and slaying the dragon. The image demonstrates the identification of these two figures – of El-Khader and St. George – in popular belief. In Bethlehem many houses of both Christians and Muslims have a stone relief of St. George and the dragon above their doorways.

The interest in El-Khader and St. George demonstrates that popular religion is rather persistent in preserving local traditions that are not necessarily promoted by the established religious institutions.

(Nasiri Khusru, eleventh-century pilgrim)

Muslims in front of the Dome of the Rock in Jerusalem.

CHAPTER VII

Economy and Culture in Bethlehem

Agriculture

While Bethlehem is now a modern city, the roots of its residents remain in the land, to which the people of Bethlehem have been closely connected historically. The image of Ruth gleaning in the fields of Boaz has been preserved by artists. The fertility of the fields led to the name *Bethlehem, House of Bread.* Speak of shepherds and one immediately thinks of the young shepherd David or the Bethlehem shepherds of the Christmas story. Likewise, Amos the prophet refers to himself as a shepherd and a dresser of sycamore trees.

The Olive Tree

The Arabic expression *El-Shajarah El-Mubarakah* is often used for the olive tree. It is the *blessed tree* because through it God provides so many gifts for life.

The olive tree is ideal for the environment of Bethlehem. It does not need much soil for its roots, nor does it require much water to grow. It is coniferous so that its many small leaves soak up the sunlight and produce much fruit. The nature of the olive tree is such that its lifetime spans the generations. It requires special care in the planting of its shoots and takes a long time to grow to maturity. The special nurture includes ploughing the surrounding soil and trimming the branches so that finally the tree begins to bear fruit. It is not uncommon for olive trees to be hundreds of years old.

The olive tree is symbolic of the Palestinian people's close ties to the land. The tradition is that one plants olive trees not for oneself, but for one's offspring and later descendants. Conversely, the careless destruction of an olive tree is a most grievous act because it belittles the labor of the ancestors and neglects the needs of later generations. All the more, Palestinians bemoan the enormous loss of olive trees during the years of Israeli occupation.

The olive harvest constitutes one of the most important events in the year. In September, as fruit begins to appear on the trees, people begin to make preparations and often hire watchmen who sit in watchtowers to look after the crop. The harvest process itself lasts several weeks in October. It is an affair that involves the whole familiy, so that students are given time off from school. Traditionally, people then erect tents within the olive groves where they concentrate their efforts on the harvest. The common practice is for the men to climb the trees, pick the olives from the branches and throw them down onto blankets spread on the ground to be gathered by the women.

The sacredness of the olive harvest is underscored by three things. The repeated calling upon the name of God reminds all of his grace in giving this gift. Likewise, it is customary to leave an ample number of olives on the ground for the poor to retrieve. Finally, the harvest is completed with a celebration of thanksgiving. This practice goes back to Canaanite times and was adopted by the Israelites in the holiday of *Succoth*; it also spread to Europe and America in the form of the Thanksgiving Day celebrations.

Left: Farmers returning home from working in the fields.

Olive harvest.

The olive fruit itself is then eaten fresh or preserved with salt, lemon, or vinegar. Another part of the olives is taken to the olive press where oil is extracted. Large round stone olive presses are to be found throughout the area. The process involves several steps. First, a large stone wheel is pulled by a draught animal to break and smash the fruit. Then the remains are placed in bags with heavy weights squeezing out the oil. The first batch of oil is called the virgin oil and is used for cooking. Other uses include cosmetics and medicine, sacred rites, and fuel for lighting lamps.

The hulls that are left are not discarded, but are dried and used for fuel, as are twigs trimmed from the tree. Thus the olive tree provides for the people in numerous ways.

Because of the importance of the olive tree, it also provides a number of poignant symbols for life. When people are squeezed by power in times of difficulties and judgment, they are like olives in the olive press. Conversely, since the time of Noah, the olive branch has been a symbol of hope and peace.

بيت لحــم ٢٠٠٠

Olive oil factory in Beit Jala.

this area. Grapes and figs are first mentioned as characteristic of the Holy Land in literary texts written about 4,300 years ago. They are harvested in August and September and dried on the rooftops for eating year round. They became symbolic of the life of peace and prosperity: "They shall all sit under their own vines and under their own fig tree, and no one shall make them afraid" (Micah 4:4).

Pomegranates, along with grapes and figs, were mentioned by Moses as most descriptive of the Holy Land (Deuteronomy 8:8). It is not surprising that they are often represented in ancient sculpture. Almonds are harvested in early March and are a sign of the end of winter and the coming of spring. In Jeremiah 1:11-12, the almond branch symbolizes that God's words are fulfilled. Beit Jala has the reputation for having the best apricots, although they were not introduced until the Middle Ages. The types of fruits and nuts mentioned above are common in the Bethlehem area because they do not need a lot of water and are resistant to the harsh weather.

Wheat and Barley

There is a tradition that when Adam and Eve left the Garden of Eden, they took with them an ear of wheat. From archaeological excavations it appears that wheat was one of the oldest plants cultivated by humans. Thus in Iraq, kernels nearly 7,000 years old have been discovered. Likewise, barley was so prominent in the region that the ancient Sumerians used it as their basic unit of weight.

The fertile area around Beit Sahour was known for its cultivation of these crops. The biblical story of Ruth is located in that area, and residents still refer to the fields of Boaz, where Ruth gleaned in the fields for the leftover sheaves. This practice of leaving part of the harvest in the fields was common to ensure that the poor had enough to eat.

Fruits and Nuts

The people of the Bethlehem area are still primarily people of the land. A good portion have remained farmers, and the city-dwellers still have their own gardens and orchards. By caring properly for the various fruits and nuts, they are able to provide for themselves over the entire year.

Since the time when Adam and Eve made clothes of fig leaves and Noah first planted a vineyard after the great flood, grape and fig production has been prominent in

The threshing floor was also a place where generosity was evident. An old story emphasizes this attitude among Bethlehemites:

There were once two brothers: one brother was blessed with boys and girls; one had no children. Their threshing floors lay side by side, and the brother that had no children said to himself, "My brother has a large family, he needs more than I do." So during the night he took grain from his floor and put it on that of his brother. Next day the one with the large family thought, "My brother has no children. I will make him happy with more grain." I will put some for a surprise on his floor tonight." And he did so. Therefore the two brothers were blessed.

Both wheat and barley are commonly used in the baking of bread, and bread is considered the staff of life. There are several popular types of bread, including the traditional *Khobez el-Tabun* made in clay ovens.

Harvesting and binding ears of corn: traditional work in the fields. Right: Khobez el-Tabun.

بيت لحـــم ٢٠٠٠

Industry

As modern cities, Bethlehem, Beit Sahour, and Beit Jala are economically dependent upon the industry of a variety of factories. These include textiles and food products, such as a noodle factory in Beit Sahour.

The Bethlehem area is situated in what was in biblical times called the hill country of Judea. The limestone hills are covered with only a thin layer of soil and vegetation so that large masses of stone are exposed and visible to the visitor. This stone has become an important natural resource.

The largest quarries in the West Bank are found in the Bethlehem area. Many of the oldest quarries have been covered and built over. Such is the case in the Moradeh area north of the Church of the Nativity along the road to Rachel's Tomb. Other quarries are spread throughout the area.

Because of traditional aesthetics, traditional preference, and the environment, all homes are constructed of stone. The stone cutting industry is therefore one of the oldest in the Bethlehem region. However, in the last 30 years, the style of stone cutting has changed with the development of new electric saws. It is now common to cut thinner stones for the facades of buildings. But even with the latest techniques and machinery, the old techniques of stone carving with chisel and hammer are still considered an art which cannot be replaced.

The Slayyib quarry in Beit Jala is most distinctive because it produces a rose-colored stone. This is probably the source of the stone for the columns in the Church of the Nativity. In 1958, red stone columns were extracted for the building of the Hashemite Palace in Baghdad.

Today more than half of the stone quarried in the Bethlehem area is exported to Israel. Other Arab states and especially the Gulf states prefer Bethlehem stone for building.

Because residents have traditionally been farmers, the art of terrace building has been practiced for centuries to prevent erosion and to maximize the utilization of the already sparse amount of soil for growing. The stone terraces along the hillsides remain a beautiful sight.

Page 112 and 113: Shepherds in the Bethlehem area.

Right: Stone-cutting workshop in Bethlehem.

Left: People at their everyday work.

Mother-of-Pearl and Olive Wood Sculpture

One of the most successful industries in the Bethlehem area is the making of mother-of-pearl. This industry, of course, is not native to the area. The material resources at first came from the Red Sea and today come from New Zealand.

It is likely that the artistic technique was introduced by the Franciscans, who invited artists from Italy in the fourteenth century. One Franciscan of the late sixteenth century, Father Bernard Amico, is well known for having made miniature reproductions of churches out of mother-of-pearl. More common were – and still are – rosaries, crosses, and jewelry boxes.

The carving of olive wood is more natural to the area because of the abundance of olive trees. St. Francis is said to have introduced the first nativity crèche in his home town of Assisi. It is only natural that this art was also introduced by the Franciscans, who then taught the wood-carving craft in their vocational schools. The mixture of dark and light wood grains has made this type of sculpture especially popular.

Both the mother-of-pearl and olive-wood-carving industries are related to the tourist industry and the presence of a large number of pilgrims in Bethlehem. At the same time, they have also been important sources of exports. There are reports of exhibitions of these products at world fairs in the latter part of the nineteenth century and various Bethlehemites are known to have traveled to Brazil, Mexico, and the United States to set up an international business network.

Worker in a candle factory. Candles are a popular souvenir from Bethlehem.

بيت لحــم ٢٠٠٠

Handling mother-of-pearl has a long tradition in Bethlehem; it came from Damascus between the fourteenth and sixteenth cen-turies. Mother-of-pearl is pre-dominantly used for intarsia work. This picture is a drawing by Charles Wilson (1865).

Tourism

Bethlehem has always been known for its hospitality, from the days of the pilgrim visitors of the Middle Ages to the growth of modern tourism.

One million visitors came to Bethlehem in the year 1995 alone. This is an average of 50 tour buses a day. But the economic impact of tourism at that time was minimal since visitors stayed an average of only 45 minutes, while spending extensive time in Israel. This has been the predominant pattern because tourism has been dependent upon the Israeli Tourist Authority.

With Palestinian autonomy, Bethlehem now has its own tourist authority which is working to restore the successful traditions of pre-1967 Bethlehem, while at the same time promoting progressive ideas like the *Bethlehem 2000* project.

30 years of Israeli occupation placed heavy obstacles against the development of a once-thriving Palestinian tourist industry. Without permits, there were no new hotels while the Israelis built hundreds. The number of Arab-owned tourist agencies has declined while the number of Israeli agencies has increased to a figure twelve times as large. Regulatory restrictions have made it impossible for licensed Arab tour guides to be replaced after retirement so that their number has fallen to about 50. In contrast, the number of Israeli guides is now in excess of 4,000.

Palestinian autonomy provides for the development of tourism and the city of Bethlehem has taken the lead.

It was no accident that popular Elias Freij, longtime mayor of Bethlehem, was the first Palestinian Minister of Tourism.

In Bethlehem several new hotels have already been constructed since 1995 and new tourist agencies organized. Bethlehem University provides courses in hotel management so that a new generation will be ready to embrace a restored tourist trade. Likewise several top-notch courses have been developed for potential guides.

These efforts in tourism have already yielded a positive response: the International Center of Bethlehem received an award for socially responsible tourism by the International Tourism Fair at its 1997 conference in Berlin.

The *Bethlehem 2000* project has mobilized resources for the promotion of an influx of tourists and pilgrims. The refurbishing of Manger Square provides an atmosphere that allows visitors to feel at home in Bethlehem. The potential is great enough to give Israelis and Palestinians the opportunity to unite for a common goal. The Palestinians of Bethlehem have much to offer: a city with close historic and spiritual roots with nearby Jerusalem, the Bethlehem region rich in history and beauty, and the heritage of its own residents with their spirit of hospitality.

An open and unrestricted tourist trade will surely contribute, not only to the economy of Bethlehem, but also to the peace process in general.

Left: Olive wood workshop and religious souvenirs. The olive-wood-carving craft was brought to Bethlehem by Franciscans in the fourteenth century. There are over 100 workshops for mother-of-pearl and olive-wood-carving articles in town. Among the most common products are biblical figures, mangers and small articles for everyday use.

Music, Song and Dance

As in the rest of Palestine, in Bethlehem there is a close relationship between music, singing and dancing, thus merging different elements into an artistic unity. Popular festivities with singing but no dancing are relatively rare and, likewise, dancing generally takes place in a setting with other musical offerings.

Palestinian musical instruments consist of stringed, wind and rhythm instruments. The most important stringed instruments are the "ud" (Arab lute), the "rebabe" (one-stringed instrument) and the "qanum" (a kind of zither). The most common instruments are the "naiy", the "midshwis" (single and double flutes), the "shababe" (like a metal recorder) and the "urghul" (consisting of two pipes of different length). The most common rhythm instruments are the "durbaka" (conic drum with ceramic body), the "tabl" (normal drum) and the "daft" (tambourine).

In Palestine folk-dances are most often performed on joyful occasions, for example at popular festivities, weddings and religious festivals. The "dabke", the most well-known Palestinian folk-dance, is performed to tunes played on the "midshwis", the "urghul" or the "shababe". The dancers form an open circle, led by the "lawih". He waves a cloth and guides them by moving his eyes and hands. The dance begins with a solo played on one of these instruments. Then the "qawil", the group singer, starts up and the group begins making light, repetitive rhythmic movements with their feet, speeding up soon as directed. Now the group begins to move around the musician with skillful steps, maintaining the circle, whereas the "lawih" occasionally separates from the group and moves freely in accordance with the given rhythm. The musician and the singer keep on playing and singing.

During the performance dancers slow down, then speed up as the song requires. The lyrics often greatly influence the stirrings of emotion and the speed of steps, thrilling the watchers and encouraging them to join in. In northern Palestine men and women dance the "dabke" together, while in other regions women form circles of their own.

As in the whole Arab world, in Palestine there are rarely musical performances without solos or everyone joining in. The reason is that Arabs attach great importance to the spoken word and there is a rich fund of poems that have influenced Arab sentiments, the arts in general, and music and song in particular. That also applies to the Palestinian folk-song.

Most Palestinian melodies are relatively simple in their musical structure and include many refrains. This heightens the artistic feeling of musicians, singers, dancers and listeners. The singers sometimes depart from the given tune and, on the basis of the rhythm and underlying beat, add their own ornamental improvisation.

Page 122: Palestinian farmer woman in traditional dress (photograph taken in 1870). The hat adorned with gold and silver coins (shatweh), topped by a veil (tarbia), symbolize her status as a married woman.

Page 123: Palestinian embroidered dress. People still wear these dresses during festivities, especially in the rural area surrounding Bethlehem. The top (kabbeh) contains different geometrical ornaments embroidered with colorful silk threads. Bethlehem is famous for its beautiful embroidery.

Above: The Old Bethlehem Home. The Women's Association of Bethlehem has established a museum in one of the oldest houses in town. There the Palestinian traditional way of life is shown in five exhibition rooms (for example living room, bedroom, kitchen). Tools and household articles are also on show.

Right: Flute-player.

Dabke folk-dance group.

Young Palestinian women at a political rally near Abu Ghuneim
(Har Homa).

Palestinian policewoman.

CHAPTER VIII

The Political Situation in Bethlehem since 1995

The Oslo Peace Accords

On the evening of December 21, 1995, autonomy (self-government) came to Bethlehem. With a quiet and simple ceremony handing over the authority to the Palestinian police, Israeli forces departed the city for the first time in 28 years and the residents of Bethlehem were left to determine their own future after so long under foreign – namely Ottoman, British, Jordanian, and Israeli – rule.

The introduction of autonomy was accompanied by midnight celebrations in Manger Square, the arrival of Palestinian police, the raising of the Palestinian flag, and, several days later, Chairman Yasser Arafat's first Bethlehem speech. The coming of autonomy marked a new beginning characterized by the hope and joy of the first Christmas celebrated under the direction of the people of Bethlehem.

Yasser Arafat with the Greek Orthodox patriarch during Christmas celebrations in Bethlehem.

*Demonstration against the Israeli
occupying power during the
Intifada.*

Autonomy for Bethlehem is one small part of the Middle East Peace Accords which consist of three major agreements: The results of the Madrid Peace Conference in October 1991, the *Declaration of Principles* signed September 13, 1993 (Oslo I) and the *Israeli-Palestinian Interim Agreement* signed September 28, 1995 (Oslo II).

The **Madrid Peace Conference**, co-chaired by the United States and the Soviet Union, was based on the principles of United Nations Security Council Resolutions 242 and 338 for the return of land occupied by Israel in 1967 in exchange for peace between Israel and its neighbors. This conference was only the opening for numerous bilateral discussions between Israel and the Palestinians, Jordan, Syria, and Lebanon. Afterwards, working groups were established on key issues of regional concern: economic development, refugees,

water, environment, arms control, and regional security. This has led to a number of agreements signed by Israel and its neighbors.

Oslo I: Under the leadership of Norway's foreign minister Johan Jorgen Holst, private discussions between the PLO and Israel produced the *Declaration of Principles* (Oslo I) which focused on the mutual recognition between the PLO and Israel. The question of mutual recognition had been a major obstacle to peace since the PLO covenant had denied Israel's right to exist and, on the other hand, Israeli law made it a crime to talk with members of the PLO. The breakthrough was symbolized by the famous handshake between Yitzhak Rabin and Yasser Arafat at the September 13, 1993 signing ceremony on the White House lawn.

This agreement was built on the principle of mutual trust so that future negotiations would lead to constructive agreements. The signing parties agreed to "put an end to decades of confrontation and conflict, recognize their mutual legitimate and political rights, and strive to live in peaceful coexistence and mutual dignity and security to achieve a just, lasting and comprehensive peace settlement and historic reconciliation".

Thus the more difficult questions were to be put off until later – at first this was projected until 1996, then postponed until 1998, and then postponed again – with the permanent status negotiations concerning borders, security arrangements, Israeli settlements, refugees, and Jerusalem. The trust-building arrangement of interim self-government, however, was set in motion by Oslo I and then finalized in the Cairo Agreement of May 1994. The intention was the immediate withdrawal of Israeli troops from Jericho and Gaza and the establishment of the Palestinian Authority.

The transfer of authority in the West Bank affected not only territory but also domestic concerns such as education, culture, health, social welfare, and tourism. By August 1995, agreements had been signed transferring authority concerning agriculture, census and statistics, energy, insurance, labor, local government, postal services, trade and industry, and taxation.

The main source of revenue for the Palestinian Authority initially came from taxes paid by Palestinians, but collected and forwarded by the Israeli government. The Palestinian Monetary Authority was established to oversee the local banking system using Israeli currency. Oslo I called attention to the key role of economic development in Palestine for the success of the peace process. This requires close cooperation between the Israeli government and the Palestinian Authority. It also depends heavily on world support. Although trade relations with other countries continued to be determined by Israeli policies, the Ministry of Planning and International Cooperation worked with the World Bank so that free trade agreements were made with the United States, the European Union, and several other countries. Donor nations met to provide economic support for a five-year period from 1993-98 for infrastructure and capital for economic development. An

amount of over three billion dollars was pledged at that time with the major support (over 200 million dollars each) coming from the United States, the European Union, the European Investment Bank, Japan, Saudi Arabia, and the World Bank. While this commitment is impressive, the total five-year figure of all donor states is put into perspective by the fact that it is not larger than the annual financial commitment by the United States alone to Israel.

The **Israeli-Palestinian Interim Agreement** (Oslo II) of September 1995 provided details for the territorial expansion of the Palestinian Authority and the extent of control given to it. This document divided the West Bank into three zones: Area A comprises three percent of the area of the West Bank, but includes major population centers of Tulkarem, Qalqilya, Jenin, Nablus, Ramallah, Bethlehem, Jericho, and Hebron. Israeli military redeployment was carried out in the fall of 1995 for the first six of these cities culminating in the Christmas celebration in Bethlehem. Subsequent developments led to the postponement of redeployment for Hebron until January, 1997. Area A is controlled by the Palestinian Authority.

Area B comprises 25 percent of the area of the West Bank and includes 450 Palestinian towns and villages. Joint patrols were established for these areas so that the Palestinian police force is responsible for public order while the Israeli army retains what is called "overriding responsibility for security". The number of Palestinian police was set with a maximum of 12,000 in the West Bank and 18,000 in Gaza.

Area C comprises 72 percent of the West Bank which includes Israeli settlements, areas with lower Palestinian population density, agricultural land, nature reserves, the Jordan Valley, and designated military areas. Israel retains full control in Area C.

This territorial division affects Bethlehem as follows: an eight-square-kilometer area of the city of Bethlehem was designated Area A, parts of the surrounding towns Beit Jala, Beit Sahour, and a number of villages were Area B, and the remainder of the Bethlehem region was Area C including Rachel's Tomb, the Etzion block of settlements to the south, the summit of Beit Jala, and the Herodium.

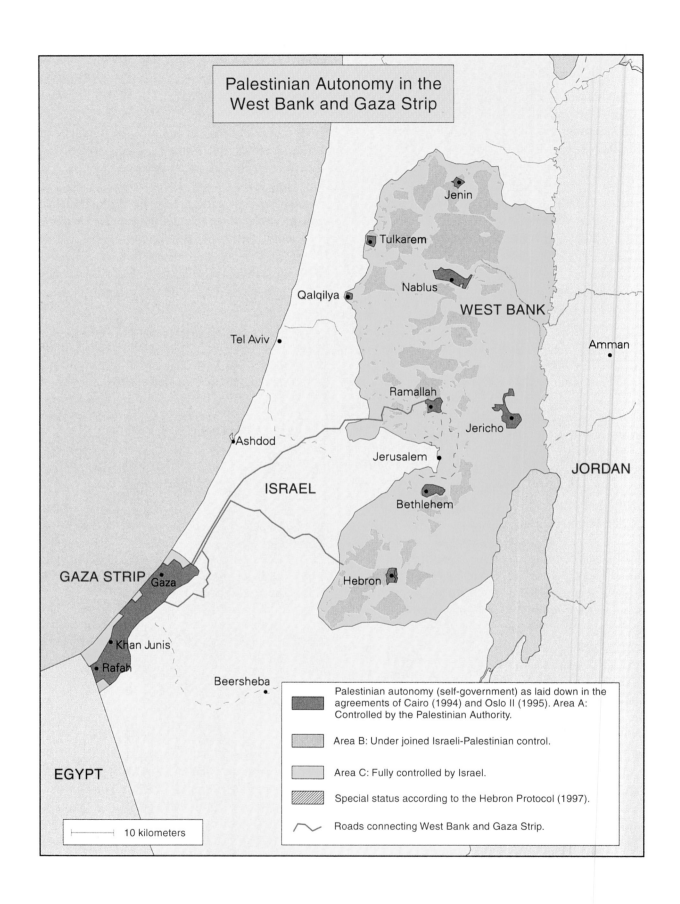

Palestinian Autonomy in the
West Bank and Gaza Strip

Jenin

Tulkarem

Qalqilya

Nablus

WEST BANK

Tel Aviv

Amman

Ramallah

Jericho

Ashdod

Jerusalem

ISRAEL

JORDAN

Bethlehem

GAZA STRIP Gaza

Hebron

Khan Junis

Rafah

Beersheba

EGYPT

Palestinian autonomy (self-government) as laid down in the agreements of Cairo (1994) and Oslo II (1995). Area A: Controlled by the Palestinian Authority.

Area B: Under joined Israeli-Palestinian control.

Area C: Fully controlled by Israel.

Special status according to the Hebron Protocol (1997).

Roads connecting West Bank and Gaza Strip.

10 kilometers

بيت لحم ٢٠٠٠

Oslo II envisaged this division of territory as merely a first step, designed as a transitional phase in the further expansion of Palestinian autonomy. Thus a series of additional military redeployments were scheduled for 1996 and 1997 with Area B joined to Area A and Area C becoming Area B with the exception of about ten percent where there are Israeli settlements. With a change of government in Israel in May 1996 and the postponement of the Hebron deployment, a revised schedule of three deployments over 18 months was set to begin in 1997. None of these ever materialized so that in the summer of 1998 negotiations centered instead on a single final withdrawal from between nine and thirteen percent of the West Bank.

The impracticality of this initial stage in the long run is evident by the geographical isolation of the eight cities making up Area A. With this in mind Oslo II guaranteed "normal and smooth movement of people, vehicles, and goods within the West Bank, and between the West Bank and the Gaza Strip". The implementation of this principle, however, was not forthcoming and the territory of Area C in reality became a barrier of separation rather than a bridge. When put to the test by a period of continuing political tensions, the Israeli army initiated strict closures in both 1996 and 1997 which restricted Palestinian travel, not only to Israel proper, but also from Area A to Areas B and C and back. The issue of "safe passage" has thus dominated subsequent negotiations.

Israeli military patrol in Area C of the West Bank where the Israeli army retains military control after the Oslo II Agreement.

بيت لحــم ٢٠٠٠

Elections

The Oslo II Agreement provided for a democratic government centered around the democratically elected Palestinian Legislative Council (88 members) and its president. In order to assure a fair representation of all religious groups, a quota was introduced. Two of Bethlehem's four mandates were reserved for Christians; there were also to be two Christian representatives from Jerusalem, one from Ramallah, and one from Gaza City. Likewise one seat from Nablus was reserved to represent the Samaritan minority.

The first elections were held on January 20, 1996 under the eye of an international team of election observers. A total of 674 candidates stood for the 88 legislative seats, among them 33 candidates for the four Bethlehem seats. In the Bethlehem area, 75 percent of eligible voters turned out to participate in this first national election – a larger number than the 68 percent figure for all of Palestine. Of these, 89 percent, slightly higher than the national average, cast their vote for Yasser Arafat as the first Palestinian President. The success of these first elections was widely interpreted as an endorsement for democratic government and for the peace process in general.

Military Checkpoint

Bethlehem is separated from Jerusalem by an Israeli military checkpoint on the Jerusalem-Hebron road near the Ecumenical Study Center of Tantur. The checkpoint had been utilized only sporadically prior to the opening of the peace talks in 1991. Since the Madrid Peace Conference, it has become a permanent fixture providing daily humiliation for Palestinians traveling to Jerusalem. Likewise the number of those permitted passage to Jerusalem has been severely limited.

This creates numerous difficulties from a historical, economic, and religious point of view. Historically many of the finer homes built along the Hebron Road, especially in the al-Baqah quarter of Jerusalem, were constructed and owned by Bethlehem residents until

they were confiscated and incorporated into West Jerusalem during the 1948 war. Bethlehemites still have close family ties with East Jerusalem. Bethlehem and Jerusalem are economically interdependent, with thousands of Palestinians employed in the Jerusalem area and natural resources and food produce coming from the Bethlehem area. Both Christians and Muslims see Jerusalem as central to their religious life, where prayers are said at the Church of the Holy Sepulchre and the El-Aqsa Mosque.

Since the beginning of Israeli military occupation in 1967, Bethlehemites have been restricted from visits to any part of Jerusalem without special permission. Because of the centrality of Jerusalem in location, it is extremely difficult for Palestinians to travel to other parts of the West Bank or to Gaza, as well as to the Ben Gurion airport. A system of careful screening allows qualified persons as exceptions to the rule and travel permits are issued to them, which must be renewed periodically.

Palestinians see these checkpoints as a barrier to their livelihood and to the rights of humanity. The checkpoints are places where many with permits suffer daily humiliation. In an inconsistent manner, blue-plated Palestinian vehicles are stopped while yellow-plated Israeli cars are allowed to pass freely. The Israelis still possess the right to close Jerusalem to Palestinians unilaterally. In the first two years following the establishment of Palestinian autonomy in May 1994, there were 25 closures of Jerusalem for varied periods of time.

Bethlehemites also fear a gradual erosion of territory with the checkpoints moving further to the south. From 1948 to 1967, the border to West Jerusalem stood near the Mar Elias Monastery. In 1991, the checkpoint was established at Tantur. In 1996, with Bethlehem under Palestinian autonomy, a second checkpoint was established at Rachel's Tomb. In 1994, the Jerusalem city council declared some of the Bethlehem area to be part of Greater Jerusalem and potentially subject to further expansion.

Above right: The military checkpoint north of Bethlehem on the road to Jerusalem.

Below right: Israeli soldiers checking identity cards.

Prior to Oslo I, one third of the Palestinian work force – totaling about 120,000 people – had employment within Israel. For Bethlehemites, who were employed mostly in nearby Jerusalem, the figure is closer to 50 percent. Thus Oslo II called for a commitment that "both sides will attempt to maintain the normality of movement of labor between them, subject to each side's right to determine from time to time the extent and conditions of labor movement into its area". However, the spirit of this principle was soon lost so that within two years the number of permits for work within Israel had been reduced to 29,000. The economic impact on cities like Bethlehem has been devastating with unemployment reaching 40-50 percent.

The effect of closures has compounded the devastation. In 1996 and 1997 alone, the total number of days of complete closure numbered 235 or 31 percent of the time. The World Bank estimates the cost of such closures at 13.6 million dollars per day since it means also a lack of import of supplies and a lack of export of goods in addition to the loss of workers' daily wages. This is equivalent to a figure of over three billion dollars during this two-year period. In effect then, the closures have offset the impact of the financial investment from donor nations – which is also around three billion dollars.

the finest homes west of the old city, especially in the al-Baqah quarter.

The 1948 War, however, resulted in a divided city. The military confrontation in West Jerusalem, the expulsion of the Arabs, and the appropriation of Bethlehem-owned homes and businesses severed those historic roots. Yet Bethlehem's attachment to East Jerusalem grew stronger than ever. Health, education, and social welfare networks of the two cities were closely linked. Business thrived, especially the tourist industry which brought pilgrims from around the world to the Holy Land and showed them the meaning of hospitality.

War again worked to sever those ties in 1967. Although Israel conquered both Bethlehem and East Jerusalem, a wedge was driven between them to make their separation permanent. Annexation and redrawn boundaries served to produce a Jewish majority for the Holy City. The result is that military road blocks and a system of permits now make it difficult for Bethlehemites to go to work, to attend school, to receive medical care, or to visit family in nearby Jerusalem. On Good Friday and Easter, Christians from Bethlehem are no longer able to pray at the Church of the Holy Sepulchre, nor are the Muslims from the West Bank and the Gaza Strip allowed to pray in the El-Aqsa Mosque in Jerusalem during the month of Ramadan.

The Status of Jerusalem

The Oslo Peace Accords have placed the issue of Jerusalem under the final status negotiations. This decision, too, has had a critical impact on the residents of Bethlehem.

In 1947, the United Nations partition plan declared that Jerusalem was to be an international city, demilitarized and open equally to people of three faiths: Judaism, Islam, and Christianity. At the time, the population was evenly divided among Arabs and Jews. Recognizing the historic, geographic, and spiritual ties, the boundaries of Jerusalem were drawn to include also Bethlehem. This was more than symbolic. Residents of Bethlehem had invested heavily in the economic development of Jerusalem and built some of

بيت لحم ٢٠٠٠

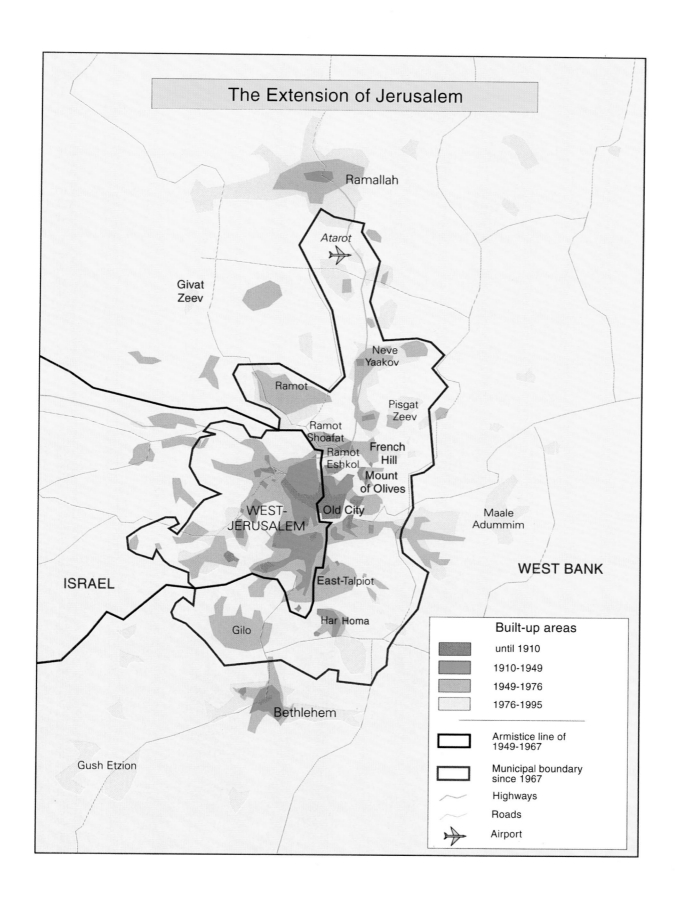

The Extension of Jerusalem

Built-up areas

until 1910

1910-1949

1949-1976

1976-1995

Armistice line of
1949-1967

Municipal boundary
since 1967

Highways

Roads

Airport

Settings

One of the most difficult issues facing the people of Bethlehem is that of the Jewish settlements. Within the Bethlehem district alone there are 18 settlements, and another three are positioned just to the north at the southern edge of the city of Jerusalem. Although these Bethlehem settlements include a population of only approximately 10,000 people (the Gilo settlement near Jerusalem, however, has a population of 60,000), they have expropriated over half the land, use a high proportion of natural resources, and pose a security threat for Palestinians.

The situation of the town of Beit Jala is a good example since it is almost completely surrounded by settlements. To the west of Beit Jala is the green line, the border with Israel itself since 1948. Even that distance has been shortened with the establishment of the Har Gilo settlement on the summit of Ras Jala. Across the valley to the north is the large Gilo settlement which is near Jerusalem and, according to Israeli understanding, part of it. To the south is the Etzion block of settlements. As if that were not enough, the new by-pass road for the Israeli settlers cuts across Beit Jala land and leads through a tunnel underneath the town.

The Gilo settlement between Jerusalem and Bethlehem. Israeli settlements often rise above Palestinian villages and towns like fortresses.

بيت لحــم ٢٠٠٠

The situation of Beit Jala is representative of that of the Bethlehem district as a whole. The settlement plan envisages surrounding the entire area with settlements so that Bethlehem is virtually cut off from Hebron in the south, Arab East Jerusalem in the north, and the rest of the West Bank. Bethlehem falls under Palestinian autonomy, yet it will be a canton separate from the rest of Palestine.

The settlement issue has been described as the most serious obstacle to peace in the Holy Land. It is a violation of international law. According to Article 49 of the Fourth Geneva Convention "the occupying power shall not deport or transfer parts of its own civilian population into the territory it occupies." Likewise United Nations Resolution 452 in 1979 calls on Israel to "cease, on an urgent basis, the establishment, construction and planning of settlements in the Arab territories occupied since 1967, including Jerusalem".

The strategic plan to settle the West Bank originated immediately after the 1967 War. Six settlements were built in the Bethlehem area under an Israeli Labor government during the first decade after the 1967 War. In the next 15 years under the Likud government, another twelve were established. On the whole, settlements flourished at this time with a 23-fold increase in the number of West Bank settlers and the escalation of financial incentives and support for settlements; soon 20 percent of the Israeli housing budget were designated for settlements. By 1982, 55 percent of the West Bank had been declared *State Land* and designated for settlement use.

Following the 1991 Madrid Peace Conference, the Labor party was voted into power in 1992 with a platform declaring a freeze on West Bank settlements. By the end of 1993, however, some areas of the Bethlehem district were declared to be part of Greater Jerusalem and thus exempt from this freeze. Since the Madrid Peace Conference, the rate of land confiscation has actually increased 400 percent and settler population has increased 25 percent. In particular, the Gush Etzion block of settlements south of Bethlehem has continued to expand. Since its coming to power in June 1996, the position of the Likud government under Prime Minister Netanyahu has been one of active and public support for the expansion of settlements.

Some of the Jewish settlers are living in the West Bank for religious and some for economic reasons. According to a recent poll, over half of the settlers would relocate in Israel if given the same financial incentives. It is reported that settlers enjoy the advantage of a considerable income tax deduction, land purchase at five percent of actual land value, interest-free or low-interest loans, and a 19,000 dollar housing grant, in addition to provisions for schools and social programs.

According to the 1994 Cairo Agreement, the settlements remain exempt from rule of the Palestinian Authority and continue to have their own system of laws and their own infrastructure. This makes for a dual system similar to apartheid. The settlements have their own road system. The 25-kilometer highway through the Bethlehem area connects the Etzion block with Jerusalem. It further isolates Palestinian communities and is partly off limits for Palestinian drivers.

Israeli and Palestinian peace groups demonstrating against the Israeli settlement plan at Abu Ghuneim (Har Homa). On the mountain ridge in the background, the Mar Elias Monastery.

In 1995, approval was given for an entirely new settlement at Abu Ghuneim, neighboring Bethlehem and Beit Sahour. This settlement, called *Har Homa,* is to occupy 400 acres of land belonging to Beit Sahour and Bethlehem residents. The plan projects 8,000 housing units for a settlement population of around 40,000. In addition, the plan ignores the concerns of environmentalists since the project will destroy one of the few forests in the Bethlehem area. Likewise, it raises religious issues since the Mar Elias Monastery is nearby, as are the remains of the ancient Abu Ghuneim and Bir el-Qutt monasteries.

The Control of Water

Today there is a common myth shared with tourists that modern Israel has converted the Palestinian desert into a green and luscious oasis. In reality, this misconstrues the hard and painful experience of life under occupation and the inequitable management of water resources.

The control of water is one of the most crucial issues in the Middle East and is inseparable from the Israeli-Palestinian conflict over land. In fact, water resources have been one of the major causes of war.

The 1967 War, which led to the military occupation of Bethlehem and all of the West Bank, was caused in part by a desire to control the various regional water resources. Throughout occupation, all water resources were declared state property by military order. Even following the Oslo Peace Accords, the West Bank water remains under the control of the Israeli civilian administration.

The reality today concerning water is as follows: 80 percent of West Bank water resources are either used by Jewish settlements or directed to Israel proper. As a result, Palestinians are allowed to use only 20 percent of their own water resources. On a per capita basis, Israel uses seven times the amount of water as do Palestinians. In addition, the cost for Palestinians is on the average three times greater than for Israelis for the same amount. The presence of West Bank Jewish settlements and their irrigated fields is a visual reminder of water inequity.

A 1992 United Nations report underscores the critical role of water:

"Water in the Occupied Territories, however limited, is largely the only natural resource Palestinians have. Any tampering with that wealth would necessarily frustrate their objective of establishing their own state and would render their claim to self-determination meaningless."

Refugees

Over the centuries, many people have sought refuge in Bethlehem for a number of reasons including war, famine, economic hardship, and other unfortunate circumstances. According to the Gospel of Luke, it was ultimately the imposition of a harsh Roman regime (by way of the census it imposed) that brought Joseph and Mary to Bethlehem when Jesus was born.

The issue of refugees is a long-standing and unresolved problem of the Arab-Israeli conflict. Before 1948, 800,000 Palestinians lived behind the green line. After the war, only 100,000 stayed behind, continuing to live there as citizens of Israel. Most of those who left did not have a choice, since 480 Arab villages were completely destroyed and the right of return was denied, while the Israeli state enacted the right of return for Jews. This was contrary to United Nations Resolution 194, adopted in December 1948, that recognized the right of return for Palestinians.

Many of the refugees fled to Jordan, Syria, and Lebanon. Others were absorbed into West Bank communities such as the Bethlehem area. Yet others declared refugee status and were housed in 27 refugee camps in the West Bank and the Gaza Strip. With the 1967 War, there were further refugees. The fact that these refugee camps, with a current population of 475,000, continue to exist five decades later is one of the greatest tragedies of the twentieth century.

Bethlehem has three such refugee camps. The largest is Dheishah camp, which is located to the south of Bethlehem on the east side of the Hebron Road. This camp was originally intended as a temporary shelter for about 1,000 residents. In fact, the name *Dheishah* means *A Splendor of Greenery,* and the site was a favorite leisure spot for Bethlehemites. The tents were soon replaced with make-shift semi-permanent housing, and the community developed into a homogenous neighbor-hood characteristic of crowded urban centers. Today there are 8,700 residents of the Dheishah camp. Apart from Dheishah there are two more refugee camps in Bethlehem. The Aidah camp is located on the west side of the Hebron Road near Rachel's Tomb. Today it has 3,300 residents. The Beit Jibrin (Azeh) camp between the Hebron Road and the new road leading into Bethlehem has about 1,500 residents.

The United Nations Relief and Works Agency for Palestine Refugees in the Near East (UNRWA) is responsible for the refugee camps. It has its own schools and vocational programs. The UNRWA provides health and rehabilitation services. It is also responsible for water, electricity, and sanitation.

Below and right: Dheishah refugee camp.

بيت لحـــم ٢٠٠٠

Psalms for Refugees

A Jewish Psalm (Psalm 137)

By the rivers of Babylon –
There we sat down and there we wept
When we remembered Zion.
On the willows there
We hung up our harps.
For there our captors
Asked us for songs,
And our tormentors asked for mirth,
Saying, "Sing us one of the songs of Zion!"
How could we sing the Lord's song
In a foreign land?
If I forget you, O Jerusalem,
Let my right hand wither!
Let my tongue cling to the roof of my mouth,
If I do not remember you,
If I do not set Jerusalem
Above my highest joy.

A Palestinian Psalm

By the hillside of Dheishah –
There we sat down and there we wept
When we remembered our villages.
On the olive branches there
We hung up our stringed uds.
For there our captors
Asked us for songs,
And our tormentors asked for mirth,
Saying, "Sing us one of the songs of your village!"
How could we sing the Lord's song
In a foreign land?
If I forget you, my homeland,
Let my right hand wither!
Let my tongue cling to the roof of my mouth,
If I do not remember you,
If I do not set my homeland
Above my highest joy.

Emigration

The problem of emigration is a very serious issue that has faced the residents of Bethlehem throughout the twentieth century.

In 1908 when the Turks began to draft Christians into the army, residents of Beit Jala and Bethlehem were among the first to emigrate. There had been others who had left earlier for economic reasons as part of a great wave of emigration during the last part of the nineteenth century. It has been estimated that well over a million persons from the Ottoman Empire emigrated to the Americas between 1860-1914. However, the number of Christians emigrating from the Bethlehem area seems especially large. It is estimated that the Christians originally from Bethlehem and Beit Jala now living abroad number 150,000, while those still residing in the Bethlehem area number only 25,000.

There are numerous success stories from emigrants to Chile, Brazil, Honduras, and the United States. The Jarur Brothers Cotton Factory in Chile is one of the most striking examples. Some were so successful that they returned with their fortunes to construct beautiful homes such as that of Sulaiman Jacir on Hebron Road. Abdul Majid Shuman, who left Bethlehem in 1911 with eight gold pounds later returned to establish the Arab Bank. The Abdullah al-Ama brothers made their name in Egypt's cinema industry after first emigrating to the United States. However, the Citizenship Law of the British Mandate of 1925 made it extremely difficult for Palestinians to return if they had left for economic reasons.

Following the 1948 War which brought numerous refugees to Bethlehem, large numbers continued to emigrate because of the economic neglect of the West Bank by the Jordanian authorities, and the movement increased as a consequence of the Israeli occupation after 1967. Evidence of this is the fact that the total Christian population of the West Bank has not exceeded 50,000 over the last three decades when it should have doubled by natural growth.

While recent emigrants have mostly looked to the Americas where relatives are already established, many others have played important roles in the development of the Gulf States.

Today there are efforts to stem the tide of emigration affecting young people. Opportunities for high quality education such as Bethlehem University provide an alternative to foreign study programs. Likewise the International Center of Bethlehem has organized a re-integration program to assist graduates of foreign universities to contribute to the life of Bethlehem.

Today three million Palestinians live abroad while 2.2 million continue to live in the West Bank and the Gaza Strip. This demonstrates that emigration affects both Christians and Muslims. Yet it is clear that the issue is most serious for the Christian population of Bethlehem. Islamic scholar Abdel Rahman Abbad has presented a Muslim response to the phenomenon of Christian emigration:

The colors of the spectrum are seven. If one disappears, the natural order loses its balance. If one of the numbers from 0 to 10 is discarded, the whole numerical system collapses. And if one of 28 letters of the Arabic alphabet is cancelled, the whole language system loses its equilibrium... We are one nation and one people. The loss of one is the loss of the whole. This is the main reason why I look with much contempt to the emigration phenomenon and I consider it one of our national shortcomings... and more!

Right: Beit Jala. Many Christians emigrated from Beit Jala and Bethlehem to the Americas in the beginning of the twentieth century.

بيت لحم ٢٠٠٠

Bethlehem University

Bethlehem University was founded in 1973 by the Christian Brothers with the cooperation of the Roman Catholic Church to provide a quality higher education for Palestinian students. It is now one of the most important universities in the West Bank and is accredited by the Association of Arab Universities.

The 1,800 students of Bethlehem University come from various parts of the West Bank and the Gaza Strip. The B.A. degree is offered in arts, early childhood education, nursing, business administration, and hotel management. Courses are taught in both Arabic and English, and students can take foreign languages such as Hebrew, French, and Spanish. The university has a faculty of about 100 professors, including both Palestinians and expatriates.

The university library contains more than 50,000 volumes as well as a Palestinian collection. It also includes an audio-visual center.

The goal of Bethlehem University is to raise the educational level of the people of the West Bank and the Gaza Strip and to enrich the region's culture through scientific and creative activities. With high emigration rates connected to the numbers of young people studying abroad, the founders hoped that Bethlehem University would keep young, talented students contributing to their homeland.

Bethlehem 2000

The year 2000 is of major importance not only for the inhabitants of Bethlehem but for all Christians and people the world over – it ushers in the new millennium. The birth of Jesus Christ with his promise of peace, hope and redemption marks a turning-point in the history of humankind. Such an occasion calls for serious reflection on the human condition. It is time to review the past and to devise goals and guidelines for our path into the future. The Palestinian people wish to affirm that there is room in their hearts for all those who share this vision and this promise and who want to celebrate this unique event with them.

Bethlehem is currently preparing itself for the new millennium. The *Bethlehem 2000* project was established by the Palestinian Authority and declared to be an undertaking of high priority for the Palestinian people. In March 1998 a Presidential Decree set up "The Bethlehem 2000 Project Authority", comprising an international body and a Palestinian ministerial committee. The project provides for a 16-month program of events starting at Christmas 1999 and running until Easter 2001. Associated with this is a massive program for the upgrading of infrastructure, renovation of the historic city center of Bethlehem and rehabilitation of the cultural heritage of the region.

Bethlehem 2000 also presents a unique opportunity for the enhancement of the tourist industry. New guided tours and expanded facilities and programs for tourists are underway, setting the stage for the celebrations and welcoming the anticipated four million visitors.

The Bethlehemites hope to use this opportunity as the beginning of a new era for their city, their region and the world. The most important thing is not speculations about the world to come, but transforming the world of today through faith, love and hope.

The year 2000 has been for many an opportunity to dream of a new, heavenly Bethlehem, where everything will become new – from urban infrastructure to hotel accommodation. But *Bethlehem 2000* is a call for action, not for dreams.

The year 2000 is an opportunity not only for economic development, but also for spiritual growth. It was here in Bethlehem that heaven and earth met, and it should be here that people meet and communicate: residents and international visitors, Christians, Muslims and Jews, Palestinians and Israelis.

To achieve these goals Bethlehem needs justice and peace.

Mitri Raheb, Bethlehem, August 1998

بيت لحــم ٢٠٠٠

The Lord's supper. This painting by Sliman Mansour, as well as the calligraphies of Adel Nasser, are on display in the International

Center of Bethlehem. They exemplify modern Palestinian art. The Center offers a varied program of events and courses relating to Palestinian culture.

بيت لحم ٢٠٠٠

Appendix

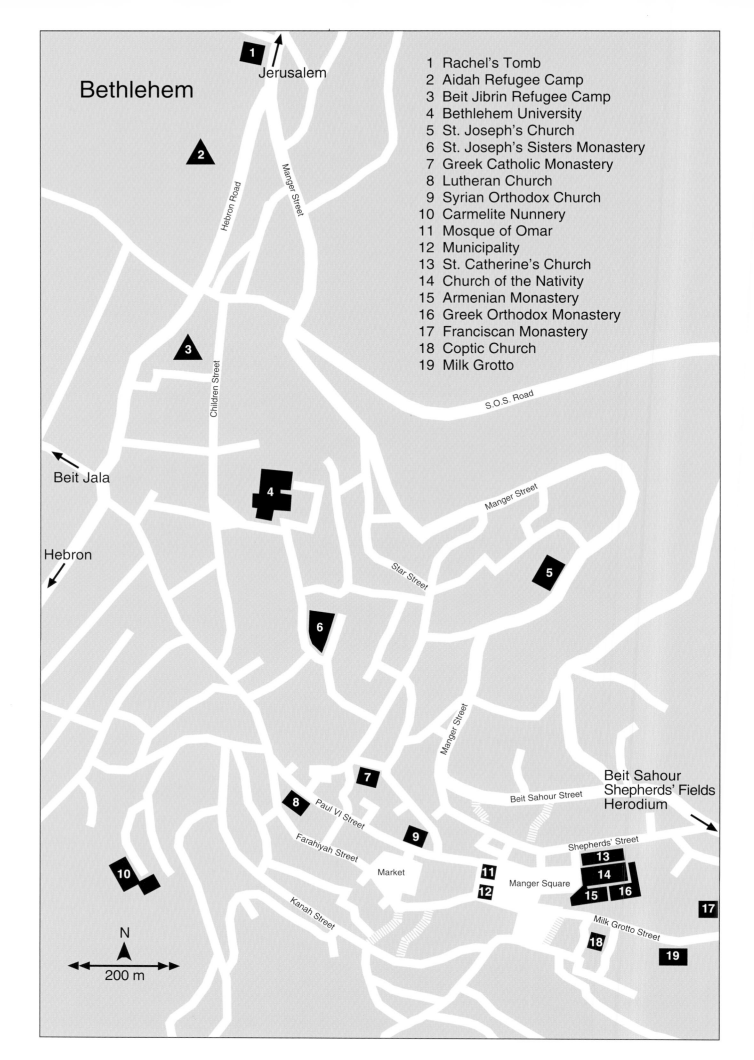

Bethlehem

1 Rachel's Tomb
2 Aidah Refugee Camp
3 Beit Jibrin Refugee Camp
4 Bethlehem University
5 St. Joseph's Church
6 St. Joseph's Sisters Monastery
7 Greek Catholic Monastery
8 Lutheran Church
9 Syrian Orthodox Church
10 Carmelite Nunnery
11 Mosque of Omar
12 Municipality
13 St. Catherine's Church
14 Church of the Nativity
15 Armenian Monastery
16 Greek Orthodox Monastery
17 Franciscan Monastery
18 Coptic Church
19 Milk Grotto

Jerusalem

Hebron Road

Manger Street

Children Street

Beit Jala

Hebron

S.O.S. Road

Manger Street

Star Street

Manger Street

Beit Sahour
Shepherds' Fields
Herodium

Beit Sahour Street

Shepherds' Street

Paul VI Street

Farahiyah Street

Market

Manger Square

Milk Grotto Street

Kanah Street

N

200 m

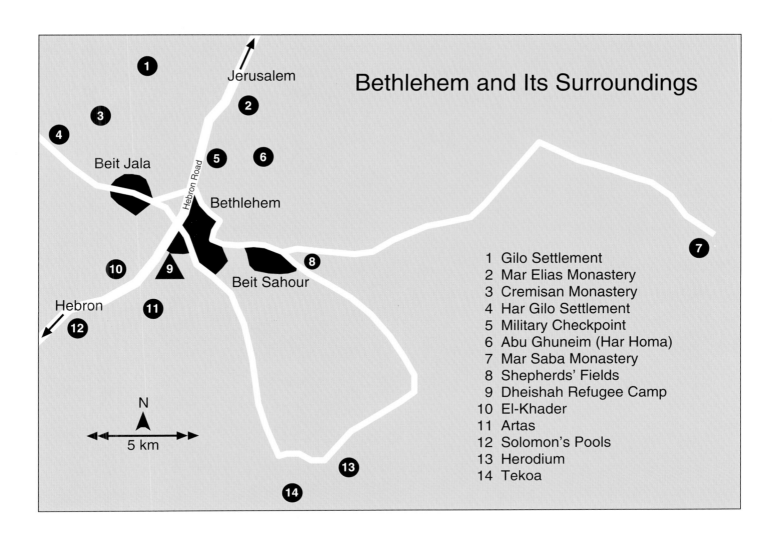

Bethlehem and Its Surroundings

1 Gilo Settlement
2 Mar Elias Monastery
3 Cremisan Monastery
4 Har Gilo Settlement
5 Military Checkpoint
6 Abu Ghuneim (Har Homa)
7 Mar Saba Monastery
8 Shepherds' Fields
9 Dheishah Refugee Camp
10 El-Khader
11 Artas
12 Solomon's Pools
13 Herodium
14 Tekoa

N

5 km

Jerusalem

Beit Jala

Hebron Road

Bethlehem

Beit Sahour

Hebron

Addresses

International

North American Coordinating Committee
of NGOs on the Question of Palestine (NACC)
1747 Connecticut Avenue, NW
Third Floor
Washington, DC 20009
Tel. 202/3190757, Fax 202/3190746
email: nacc@igc.org

Institute for Palestine Studies
3501 M Street, NW
Washington, DC 20007
Tel. 202/3423990, Fax 202/3423927
http://www.cais.net/ipsjps

Palestine Solidarity Committee
P.O. Box 539
Jamaica Plain, MA 02130

Division for Palestinian Rights
United Nations, Room S-3362
New York, NY 10017
Tel. 212/9631234, Fax 212/9634199

Palestine Solidarity Committee
BM PSA
London WCIN 3XX

Association France-Palestine
P.O. Box 184-04
75160 Paris Cedex 04

Coordination Unit for Assistance
to the Palestinian People
UNESCO
7 Place Fontenoy
75007 Paris
Tel. 01/45681899, Fax 01/45685675
http://www.unesco.org
email: o.massalha@unesco.org

European Coordinating Committee
of NGOs on the Question of Palestine (ECCP)
Rue Stevin 115
1000 Brussels
Tel./Fax 02/2310174

International Coordinating Committee
of NGOs on the Question of Palestine (ICCP)
P.O. Box 127
1211 Geneva 20

Bethlehem

Al-Liqa Center
Hebron Road
Bethlehem
Tel./Fax 02/2741639

Alternative Tourism Group
P.O. Box 173
Beit Sahour
Tel. 02/2772151, Fax 02/2772211
email: atg@p-ol.com

بيت لحم ٢٠٠٠

Alternative Information Center
Bab al-Zqaq Junction
Maraqa Building, 2. Floor
Bethlehem
Tel./Fax: 02/2747346
http://www.aic.org
email: badill@trendline.co.il

Arab Women's Union
Star Street
P.O. Box 19
Bethlehem
Tel. 02/2742453/2742589

Beit Sahour Folklore Museum
P.O. Box 56
Beit Sahour
Tel. 02/2773666

Bethlehem 2000 Project Authority
Al-Atan Street
P.O. Box 2000
Bethlehem
Tel. 02/2742224, Fax 02/2742227

Bethlehem Bibel College
Hebron Road
P.O. Box 127
Bethlehem
Tel. 02/2741190, Fax 02/2743278
http://www.bethlehembiblecollege.edu

International Center of Bethlehem
(Internationales Begegnungszentrum)
Paul VI Street
P.O. Box 162
Bethlehem
Tel. 02/2770047, Fax 02/2770048
http://www.annadwa.org
email: annadwa@Planet.edu

Municipality of Beit Jala
Al-Manshiyeh Square
P.O. Box 1
Beit Jala
Tel. 02/2742601, Fax 02/2744457

Municipality of Beit Sahour
Hai al-Baladiah Street
P.O. Box 1
Beit Sahour
Tel. 02/2773666, Fax 02/2773520

Municipality of Bethlehem
Manger Square
P.O. Box 48
Bethlehem
Tel. 02/2741323/4/5, Fax 02/2741327

Talitha Kumi
P.O. Box 7
Beit Jala
Tel. 02/2741247/2745160, Fax 02/2741847

Bethlehem University
Freres Street
P.O. Box 9
Bethlehem
Tel. 02/2741241-5, Fax 02/2744440
http://www.bethlehem.edu
email: info@bethlehem.edu

The Old Bethlehem Home
(Bethlehem Museum)
P.O. Box 19
Bethlehem
Tel. 02/2742589, Fax 02/2742453

Palestine and Bethlehem
in the Internet

PALESTINE ONLINE
http://www.p-ol.com
email: info@p-ol.com

PALESTINE-ONLINE
http://www.palestine-online.com

PALGATE
http://www.palgate.com
email: admin@palgate.com

PALNET
http://www.palnet.com
email: info@palnet.com

PLANET
Palestinian Academic Network
http://www.planet.edu

Palestine around the Web
http://www.palestine-net.com

Al-Quds
http://www.alquds.org/palestine/index.html

Birzeit University
http://www.birzeit.edu

Bibliography

Israeli-Palestinian Conflict

Abbas, Mahmoud (Abu Mazen): Through Secret Channels. The Road to Oslo, Reading 1995.

Abdel Shafi, Haider: "Moving beyond Oslo", *Journal of Palestine Studies*, vol. 25, no. 1, 1995, 76-85.

Abdullah, Samir: The Strategy of Economic Development in the Transitional Phase, in: Jerusalem Media and Communication Center (Ed.): Facing Palestinian Society in the Interim Period, Jerusalem 1994, 125-134.

Abed, George T. (Ed.): The Palestinian Economy. Studies in Development under Prolonged Occupation, London 1988.

Abu-Amr, Ziad: "Pluralism and the Palestinians", *Journal of Democracy*, vol. 7, no. 3, 1996, 83-93.

Ashrawi, Hanan: This Side of Peace. A Personal Account, New York 1995.

Asseburg, Muriel/Perthes, Volker (Ed.): The European Union and the Palestinian Authority. Recommendations for a New Policy, Ebenhausen 1998.

Avnery, Uri: "Is Oslo Dead?", *Palestine-Israel Journal*, vol. 2, no. 5, 1995, 26-32.

Avnery, Uri/Hanegbi, Haim: Who is Violating the Agreements? A Gush Shalom Research Paper, Tel Aviv 1997.

Benvenisti, Meron: Israel and the Administered Areas. West Bank Data Base Project, Jerusalem 1982.

Benvenisti, Meron: Intimate Enemies. Jews and Arabs in a Shared Land, Berkeley 1995.

Black, Ian/Morris, Benny: Israel's Secret Wars. A History of Israel's Intelligence Services, London 1991.

Corbin, Jane: Gaza First, London 1994.

Cotran, Eugene (Ed.): The Arab-Israeli Accords. Legal Perspectives, London 1996.

Dajani, Burhan: "An Alternative to Oslo?", *Journal of Palestine Studies*, vol. 25, no. 4, 1996, 5-19.

Erekat, Saeb: "What it Takes to Make Peace", *Palestine-Israel Journal*, vol. 3, no. 3-4, 1996, 18-24.

Flamhaft, Ziva: Israel on the Road to Peace. Accepting the Unacceptable, Boulder 1996.

Frangi, Abdallah: The PLO and Palestine, London 1983.

Gowers, Andrew/Walker, Tony: Behind the Myth: Yasser Arafat and the Palestinian Revolution, London 1990.

Green, Yehudit: "The Impact of Dialog", *Palestine-Israel Journal*, vol. 3, no. 3-4, 1996, 138-142.

Gresh, Alain: The PLO. The Struggle within. Towards an Independent Palestinian State, London 1988.

Halter, Marek/Laurent, Eric: Les Fous de la Paix, Paris 1994.

Hart, Alan: Arafat. A Political Biography, Bloomington 1989.

Heikal, Mohammed: Secret Channels. The Inside Story of Arab-Israeli Peace Negotiations, London 1996.

Herzberg, Arthur: "The End of the Dream of the Undivided Land of Israel", *Journal of Palestine Studies*, vol. 25, no. 2, 1996, 35-45.

Institute for Palestine Studies (Ed.): The Palestinian-Israeli Peace Agreement. A Documentary Record, London 1994.

Israeli Settlement in the West Bank. Past, Present, and Future, Alternative Information Center, Jerusalem 1995.

Jerusalem Media and Communication Center (Ed.): Facing Palestinian Society in the Interim Period, Jerusalem 1994.

Kapeliouk, Amnon: Rabbin – Un assassinat politique. Religion, nationalisme, violence en Israël, Paris 1996.

Khalidi, Rashid: "A Palestinian View of the Accord with Israel", *Current History*, vol. 93, no. 580, 1996, 62-66.

Khalidi, Walid: All that Remains. The Palestinian Villages Occupied and Depopulated by Israel in 1948, Washington 1992.

Khatib, Ghassan al-: "The Inadequacy of an Interim Agreement", *Palestine-Israel Journal*, no. 5, 1995, 13-18.

Lemarchand, Phillippe/Radi, Lamia: Israel/Palestine demain. Atlas Prospectif, 1997.

Mahler, Gregory S.: Constitutionalism and Palestinian Constitutional Development, Jerusalem 1996.

Makovsky, David: Making Peace with the PLO. The Rabin Government's Road to the Oslo Accord, Boulder 1996.

Morris, Benny: The Birth of the Palestinian Refugee Problem, 1947-1949, Cambridge 1987.

Muslih, Muhammad: "Jericho and Its Meaning. A New Strategy for the Palestinians", *Current History*, vol. 93, no. 580, 1994, 72-77.

Nassar, Jamal R./Heacock, Roger (Ed.): Intifada. Palestine at the Crossroads, New York/London 1990.

Nassar, Jamal R.: The Palestine Liberation Organization. From Armed Struggle to the Declaration of Independence, New York 1991.

Palestinian Academic Society for the Study of International Affairs/PASSIA (Ed.): The Palestinian Economy. A Bibliography, Jerusalem 1994.

Palestinian Academic Society for the Study of International Affairs/PASSIA (Ed.): PASSIA Yearbook, Jerusalem 1997.

"Palestinian Emigration", Special Issue of *Al-Liqa Journal*, no. 2, 1992.

"Palestinian Refugees and Non-Refugees in the West Bank and Gaza Strip", Special Issue of *Journal of Refugee Studies*, Oxford 1989.

Peres, Shimon: Battling for Peace. Memoirs, London 1995.

Rabin, Lea: Rabin – Our Life, His Legacy, New York 1997.

Roy, Sara M.: The Gaza Strip. The Political Economy of De-development, London 1995.

Rubinstein, Danny: The Mystery of Arafat, South Royalton 1995.

Safieh, Afif: "The Peace Process. From Breakthrough to Breakdown?", *Palestine-Israel Journal*, vol. 4, no. 1, 1997, 73-78.

Said, Edward W.: Peace and Its Discontents. Essays on Palestine in the Middle East Peace Process, London 1996.

Savir, Uri: The Process, New York 1998.

Shaat, Nabil: "A State in the Making", *Palestine-Israel Journal*, vol. 3, no. 2, 1996, 25-34.

Smith, Pamela Ann: "The Palestinian Diaspora, 1948-1985", *Journal of Palestine Studies*, vol. 15, no. 3, 1986, 91-108.

Stein, Georg: The Palestinians. Oppression and Resistance of a Disinherited People, Cologne 1988.

Strickert, Fred: "In the Shadow of the Settlements. A Farm in Palestine", *Christian Century*, April 9, 1997, 356-357.

Usher, Graham: Palestine in Crisis. The Struggle for Peace and Political Independence after Oslo, London 1995.

Wallach, Janet/Wallach, John: Arafat. In the Eyes of the Beholder, Rocklin 1992.

Zaharna, Randa S.: "A Perspective on Communication in Palestinian Society", *Palestine-Israel Journal*, vol. 3, no. 3-4, 1996, 123-128.

Ancient History

Abells, Zvi/Arbit, Asher: The City of David Water System, Jerusalem 1994.

Amit, D.: What was the Source of Herodion's Water?

Arnold, Patrick M.: Ramah, in: Freedman, David Noel (Ed.): The Anchor Bible Dictionary, vol. 5, Garden City 1992, 613-614.

Avi-Yonah, Michael/Tzaferis, Vassilios/Stekelis, M.: Bethlehem, in: Stern, Ephraim (Ed.): The New Encyclopedia of Archaeological Excavations in the Holy Land, vol. 1, Jerusalem 1993.

Axelsson, Lars: Tekoa, in: Freedman, David Noel (Ed.): The Anchor Bible Dictionary, vol. 6, Garden City 1992, 343-344.

Bagatti, B.: "Recenti scavi a Betlemme", *Liber Annuus*, no. 18, 1968, 181-237.

Bailey, Kenneth E.: "The Manger and the Inn: The Cultural Background of Luke 2:7", *Theological Review of the Near East School of Theology*, 1979, 33-44.

Benoit, P.: "Chronique Archéologique: Bethléem", *Revue Biblique*, no. 77, 1970, 583-585.

Brown, Raymond E.: The Birth of the Messiah, Garden City 1977.

Campbell, Edward F. Jr.: The Anchor Bible: Ruth, Garden City 1975.

Cazelles, Henri: Bethlehem, in: Freedman, David Noel (Ed.): The Anchor Bible Dictionary, vol. 1, Garden City 1992, 712-714.

Corbo, V.: "Herodion", *Liber Annuus*, no. 13, 1962-63, 219-277.

Corbo, V.: "Herodion", *Liber Annuus*, no. 17, 1967, 65-121.

Dothan, Trude/Dothan, Moshe: People of the Sea. The Search for the Philistines, New York 1992.

Foerster, Gideon: Herodium, in: Avi-Yonah, Michael (Ed.): Encyclopedia of Archaeological Excavations in the Holy Land, vol. 2, Englewood Cliffs 1976, 502-510.

Foerster, Gideon: Herodium, in: Stern, Ephraim (Ed.): The New Encyclopedia of Archaeological Excavations in the Holy Land, vol. 2, Jerusalem 1993, 618-621.

Hennesy, J.B.: "An Early Bronze Age Tomb Group from Beit Sahur", *Annual of the Department of Antiquities of Jordan*, no. 11, 1966, 19-40.

Keel, Othmar/Küchler, Max: Orte und Landschaften der Bibel, vol. 2, Der Süden, Göttingen 1982.

Luker, Lamonette M.: Ephrathah, in: Freedman, David Noel (Ed.): The Anchor Bible Dictionary, Garden City 1992, 557-558.

Luker, Lamonette M.: Rachel's Tomb, in: Freedman, David Noel (Ed.): The Anchor Bible Dictionary, vol. 5, Garden City 1992, 608-609.

Mazar, A.: The Aqueducts of Jerusalem, in: Jerusalem Revealed. Archaeology in the Holy City 1968-74, Jerusalem 1975, 79-84.

Netzer, Ehud: "Greater Herodium", *Qedem*, no. 13, 1981.

Netzer, Ehud: Herodium. An Archaeological Guide, Jerusalem 1987.

Netzer, Ehud: Lower Herodium, in: Stern, Ephraim (Ed.): The New Encyclopedia of Archaeological Excavations in the Holy Land, vol. 2, Jerusalem 1993, 621-626.

Saller, S.: "Iron Age Remains from the Site of a New School at Bethlehem", *Liber Annuus*, no. 18, 1968, 153-180.

Schick, Carl: "Die Wasserversorgung der Stadt Jerusalem", *Zeitschrift des Deutschen Palästina Vereins*, no. 1, 1878, 132-176.

Smith, George Adam: The Historical Geography of the Holy Land, London 1894.

Stekelis, M.: Bethlehem, in: Avi-Yonah, Michael (Ed.): Encyclopedia of Archaeological Excavations in the Holy Land, vol. 1, Englewood Cliffs 1976, 198-206.

Stockton, E.: "Stone Age Factory Site at Arafa near Bethlehem", *Liber Annuus*, no. 15, 1965, 124-30.

Stockton, E.: "The Stone Age of Bethlehem", *Liber Annuus*, no. 17, 1967, 129-148.

Tzaferis, Vassilios: Shepherds' Field, in: Stern, Ephraim (Ed.): The New Encyclopedia of Archaeological Excavations in the Holy Land, vol. 4, Jerusalem 1993, 1362-1363.

Vetrali, L.: "Le Iscrizioni Dell'Acquedotto Romano Presso Betlemme", *Liber Annuus*, no. 17, 1967, 149-161.

Welten, P.: "Bethlehem und die Klage um Adonis", *Zeitschrift des Deutschen Palästina Vereins*, no. 99, 1983, 189-203.

Religion/Christianity/Pilgrims

Ateek, Naim Stifan: Justice, and Only Justice. A Palestinian Theology of Liberation, Maryknoll 1989.

Ateek, Naim Stifan/Radford Ruether, Rosemary (Ed.): Faith and the Intifada. Palestinian Christian Voices, Maryknoll 1991.

Chitty, Derwas J.: The Desert a City. An Introduction to the Study of Egyptian and Palestinian Monasticism under the Christian Empire, Oxford 1966.

Cragg, Kenneth: The Arab Christian. A History in the Middle East, Louisville 1991.

Cyril of Scythopolis: The Lives of the Monks of Palestine, Kalamazoo 1991.

Di Segni, Leah: Life of Chariton, in: Wimbush, V. L. (Ed.): Ascetic Behavior in Greco-Roman Antiquity, Minneapolis 1990, 393-424.

Griffith, Sidnet H.: Arabic Christianity in the Monasteries of Ninth-Century Palestine, Aldershot 1992.

Hamilton, R.W.: The Church of the Nativity – Bethlehem, Jerusalem 1947.

Harvey, W.: Structural Survey of the Church of the Nativity – Bethlehem, Oxford 1935.

Hirschfeld, Yizhar: Life of Chariton in the Light of Archaeological Research, in: Wimbush, V. L. (Ed.): Ascetic Behavior in Greco-Roman Antiquity, Minneapolis 1990, 425-447.

Hirschfeld, Yizhar: Chariton, in: Stern, Ephraim (Ed.): The New Encyclopedia of Archaeological Excavations in the Holy Land, vol. 1, Jerusalem 1993, 297-299.

Hirschfeld, Yizhar: Monasteries and Churches in the Judean Desert in the Byzantine Period, in: Tsafir, Yoram (Ed.): Ancient Churches Revealed, Jerusalem 1993, 149-154.

Hirschfeld, Yizhar: The Judean Desert Monasteries in the Byzantine Period, New Haven 1995.

Horner, Norman A.: A Guide to Christian Churches in the Middle East, Indiana 1989.

Jotischky, Andrew: "Manuel Comnenus and the Reunion of the Churches. The Evidence of the Conciliar Mosaics in the Church of the Nativity in Bethlehem", *Levant*, no. 26, 1994, 207-223.

Khoury, Geries S.: Guide to the Church in the Holy Land, Nazareth 1984.

Khusru, Nasiri: Diary of a Journey through Syria and Palestine.

Patrich, Joseph: "The Hermitage of St. John the Hesychast in the Great Laura of Sabas", *Liber Annuus*, no. 43, 1993, 315-337.

Radford Ruether, Rosemary/Ruether, Herman J.: The Wrath of Jonah. The Crisis of Religious Nationalism in the Israeli-Palestinian Conflict, San Francisco 1989.

Raheb, Mitri: I am a Palestinian Christian, Minneapolis 1995.

Saller, Sylvester: The Byzantine Chapel Found at Bethlehem in 1962.

Schaff, Philip/Wace, Henry (Ed.): Jerome. A Select Library of Nicene and Post-Nicene Fathers of the Christian Church, vol. 6, Grand Rapids 1971.

"The Pilgrimage of the Russian Abbot Daniel", *The Library of the Palestine Pilgrims' Text Society*, vol. 5, New York 1971.

Vincent, L.H./Abel, F.M.: Bethléem. Le Sanctuaire de la Nativité, Paris 1914.

Bethlehem

Baannura, Tuma: Bethlehem, Beit Sahour, Beit Jala, Ephrata (Arabic), Jerusalem 1982.

Bailey, Betty Jane/Bailey, J. Martin: "Slouching Toward Bethlehem 2000", *The Link*, no. 29, 1996, 1-9.

Elalie, Giries: Bethlehem. The Immortal Town, Jerusalem 1991.

Revault, Philippe/Santelli, Serge/Weill-Rochant, Catherine (Ed.): Maisons de Bethléem, Paris 1997.

Strickert, Fred: "Religious Coexistence in a Town of Three Faces", *The Christian Science Monitor*, Dec. 24, 1996, 19.

Strickert, Fred: "Candles of Peace. In Shepherds' Fields", *Christian Century*, Dec. 24-31, 1997, 1212-1213.

Culture

Darwisch, Mahmoud: La Palestine comme métaphore, Paris 1997.

Jayyusi, Salma Khadra (Ed.): Anthology of Modern Palestinian Literature, New York 1992.

Kawar, Widad Kamel: "The Traditional Palestinian Costume", *Journal of Palestine Studies*, vol. 10, no. 1, 1980, 118-129.

Khalidi, Walid (Ed.): Before Their Diaspora. A Photographic History of the Palestinians, 1876-1948, Washington 1984.

Qleibo, Ali H.: Before the Mountains Disappear. An Ethnographic Chronicle of the Modern Palestinians, Jerusalem/Kairo 1992.

Revealing the Holy Land. The Photographic Exploration of Palestine, Santa Barbara 1997.

Weir, Shelagh: Palestinian Costume, London 1989.

Guides/Travel Books

Hamilton, R.W.: A Guide to Bethlehem, Jerusalem 1939.

Hoade, Eugene: Guide to the Holy Land, Jerusalem.

Humphreys, Andrew/Tilbury, Neil: Israel and the Palestinian Territories, Hawthorn 1996.

Murphy-O'Connor, Jerome: The Holy Land – An Archaeological Guide from Earliest Times to 1700, Oxford 1980.

Petrozzi, Maria Teresa: Bethlehem, Jerusalem 1970.

Pfeiffer, Ida: Reise einer Wienerin in das Heilige Land, Wien 1844.

Roberts, David: The Holy Land, London 1855.

Roberts, David: Yesterday and Today – The Holy Land, Vercelli/Bnei Brak 1995.

Shomali, Sawsan/Shomali, Qustandi: Bethlehem 2000. A Guide to Bethlehem and Its Surroundings, Waldbröl 1997.

Wilson, Charles W.: The Land of Judea and the Jerusalem Environs, Jerusalem n. y.